I lived some of the history recorded in this book!

Lindsborg Then
&
Lindsborg Now

Bill Carlson and Birger Sandzén painting of Bill's pioneering grandfather Magnus Carlson's "Old Homestead," in the Birger Sandzén Memorial Gallery, Lindsborg, Kansas.

Lindsborg Then & Lindsborg Now

By Bill Carlson

Outskirts Press, Inc.
Denver, Colorado

LINDSBORG THEN AND LINDSBORG NOW
Part One: Late 1860s to Early 1900s; Part Two: Year 2010

V2.0

Outskirts Press, Inc.
http://www.outskirtspress.com

ISBN: 978-1-4327-8026-5

PRINTED IN THE UNITED STATES OF AMERICA

SVHP -- ISBN 0-918331-08-X
SVHA, P.O. Box 255,
Lindsborg, KS 67456

FOREWORD

Bill "Butch" Carlson is a third-generation Smoky Valley resident whose family has now expanded to its fourth- and fifth-generations. Bill married one of the "Messiah Church girls" you will find mentioned in this book, Doris Soderstrom, the daughter of long-time Lindsborg school superintendent LaVerne "Sody" Soderstrom and his wife Amanda.

An outstanding athlete in both high school and at Bethany College, Bill went into the teaching profession and was named the first football coach of Salina South High School when it opened in 1970. Bill's sense of uncompromising fairness as a referee was very much in demand at both the high school level and in the Big 8 college conference.

In 1974, at the invitation of the institution's board of directors, Bill became administrator of Bethany Home in Lindsborg. Bill assembled a management team and staff that quite literally brought the home into the modern age.

In his retirement Bill has written several books and articles about Lindsborg and the Smoky Valley, as well as his own exceptionally interesting experiences. He also has been active in numerous projects of the Smoky Valley Historical Association. Among them is his leadership role in a project describing the location of over two dozen historical sites with signs posted along Lindsborg's Välkommen Trail as it follows the path the railroads once took though town.

With this book Carlson is striving to add to the preservation of history of Lindsborg and the Smoky Valley. He has drawn upon some of the available rich local publications, most notably the writings of celebrated Smoky Valley historian Dr. Emory Lindquist and two major tomes written in the early part of the 20th Century by the Rev. Dr. Alfred Bergin and other resources, which he acknowledges in the

Introduction. Bill also brings to bear his own valuable and insightful knowledge and understandings of the rich heritage of Lindsborg and the Smoky Valley.

The Smoky Valley Historical Association is pleased to add this book to its list of nearly a dozen books published since 1984 by the Smoky Valley Historical Publications with its editor and founder, A. John Pearson.

It is a pleasure to extend the published impact of writings by Bill Carlson.

The Smoky Valley Historical Association
2011-12 Board of Directors

Chris Abercrombie, *president*
Barbara Buskirk, *vice-president*
Marvin Johnson, *secretary*
Lenora Lynam, *treasurer*
Ken Branch
Dr. Duane Fredrickson
Julie Neywick
Richard Patrick
Chester G. Peterson

PREFACE

For a number of years we have been waiting for someone to compile research, and write about the early history of Lindsborg. Waiting, waiting! A good number of long-time residents of Lindsborg have left us, who were very capable of sharing their memories of this fine Scandinavian city.

During the 140th Anniversary of Lindsborg in 2009, we were asked by John Marshall of *The Lindsborg News-Record* to write a series of stories about the early history of our community and the Smoky Valley, here in the middle of the State of Kansas.

Further, Mrs. Linda Holmquist, representing the Wichita Area Scandinavian Association, requested a program for this group with the topic of "Lindsborg Then and Lindsborg Now." In preparation for this assignment we continued research on our community and the Smoky Valley of Kansas which was presented in early March. Further, it has occurred to me that I am now considered one of these senior citizens who may never leave some knowledge of the early history of this area. This preparation will be our contribution to the community.

Someone once said with emphasis, "History not recorded, is perhaps history lost."

Lindsborg Then deals with how Lindsborg was settled in the late 1860s, compiling data on dates, places and people primarily from the earliest books of Lindsborg, written by Dr. Alfred Bergin in the early 1900s and Dr. Emory K. Lindquist's book of 1953. *Lindsborg Now* gives the facts and impressions of Lindsborg by the writer of how this little city is today.

No attempt has been made to record history, on-going, of Lindsborg since those very early days and this year of 2010.

INTRODUCTION

For many years we have been studying and researching the early history of Lindsborg and the Smoky Valley, waiting and hoping more proficient writers will be inspired to compile and write how Lindsborg happened. And it did not just happen, as it took the dreams, planning, work, and prayers of those early settlers to make this city happen. It has been fifty-seven years since a book has been written about the early days of Lindsborg by a local resident. Swedish resident Alf Brorson of Torsby, Sweden in the province of Värmland has written numerous articles about this subject since his first visit to our community in 1993. A teacher, writer, lecturer, Mr. Brorson has publicized Lindsborg by speaking to many groups in Sweden about our community, plus has had a number of articles about the Smoky Valley in the *Sweden & America* magazine (formerly known as the *Bridge*). Mr. Brorson will be making his 17th visit to Lindsborg this coming summer where he was years ago honored by then Mayor Don Anderson as an Honorary Citizen of Lindsborg. In Swedish his latest book is *Vägen till Lindsborg* (The Road to Lindsborg) in 2010 followed by *An America Book*.

Dr. Alred Bergin's books were written in the early 1900s, and by Dr. Emory Lindquist in 1953. It must be emphasized Dr. Bergin deserves much credit for the preservation of early Lindsborg history. He not only wrote books, but also articles about early Lindsborg. He is described by Dr. Emil Lund, who served several parishes in the Smoky Valley in the 1880s, "as physically large and strong outwardly as well as inwardly, in which is found no guile, learned at home in the humanities, and especially versed in writing. A gifted speaker, spiritual guide and careful and dependable leader."

Dr. Emory Lindquist's love for the Smoky Valley is depicted in his *Smoky Valley People*, published in 1953, and later also in *A Vision for a Valley*. Dr. Lindquist, who grew up in Lindsborg, served for a number of years as President of Bethany College, and later of Wichita University. He states that "the pattern and development in Lindsborg is not the result of chance. It has its roots in devotion and faith of Swedish immigrants who came during the late mid to late 1860s to make rich contributions to the great symphony of American life — people thought, prayed, and worked together to improve the quality of living for themselves and for future generations."

Mr. A. John Pearson, retired from many years at Bethany College where his contributions to the College and Lindsborg have been priceless to our entire community, has been leader, writer, and contributor for many years to the Swedish culture of Lindsborg and the Smoky Valley. We have taken the liberty to quote John, along with those mentioned above, in this presentation of *Lindsborg Then & Lindsborg Now*.

Further, many thanks to Ms. Charlotte Ternstrom, longtime faithful secretary at Bethany Lutheran Church, for accessing and recording dates, names, and places from early church records.

And, many thanks to my wife Doris who has prevailed through many weeks of research and struggle putting all this together. She must wonder, is this any way to spend a peaceful and serene retirement?

Finally, in this attempt to preserve Lindsborg and Smoky Valley history, we must emphasize at this point, the facts, names, places, and dates have been taken from the writings of those listed above.

TABLE OF CONTENTS

Foreword v
Preface vii
Introduction ix

LINDSBORG THEN
Late 1860s to Early 1900s

Chapter 1. Dreams and Visions 3
Chapter 2. Land Agents in Sweden 5
Chapter 3. Arriving in New York, and on West to Chicago 7
Chapter 4. Land Agents in Chicago 8
Chapter 5. Settling in the Smoky Valley 10
Chapter 6. The Naming of Lindsborg 13
Chapter 7. Dugouts in the Smoky Valley 14
Chapter 8. The Hoglund Dugout 16
Chapter 9. An Early Lindsborg Community Leader 21
Chapter 10. Rev. Olof Olsson, Founder of Lindsborg 25
Chapter 11. Church Division and Controversy 27
Chapter 12. Indians in the Smoky Valley 31
Chapter 13. Another Early Smoky Valley Leader, Magnus Carlson 37
Chapter 14. Dr. Alfred Bergin 40
Chapter 15. Ellis Island 43
Chapter 16. Cooperative Farming in the Smoky Valley 45
Chapter 17. Entertainment for Pioneers in the 1860s 47
Chapter 18. Close Knit Families 49
Chapter 19. Music in the Smoky Valley 51

Chapter 20. Additional History to Be Preserved 53
Chapter 21. Traditions Continued in the Valley 55
Chapter 22. Coronado Heights 57
Chapter 23. Hobo Camps in Lindsborg 59
Conclusion of Lindsborg Then 63

LINDSBORG NOW
Year 2010

Chapter 24. Lindsborg Now in 2010 67
Chapter 25. Education in Lindsborg Always High Priority 69
Chapter 26. Celebrations 71
Chapter 27. Smoky Valley Historical Association 73
Chapter 28. Coronado Heights Today 75
Chapter 29. Lindsborg City Organizations 77
Chapter 30. Churches in Lindsborg 81
Chapter 31. Recreational Facilities 84
Chapter 32. King Carl Gustaf's Visit to Lindsborg, April 17, 1976 86
Chapter 33. Visit of the Motala Choir 89
Chapter 34. Major Happenings "Now" in 2010 91
Conclusion 95
Sources for this Presentation 98
Appendix: Doppa i Grytan Party? What Is That? 99

LINDSBORG THEN

Late 1860s to Early 1900s

Chapter 1

DREAMS AND VISIONS

As we compiled data like places, times, dates and people we were again reminded of the lack of information regarding how the city of Lindsborg became a reality 141 years ago in the late 1860s. Even though much data is available in those early books of Dr. Alfred Bergin written in the early 1900s, followed by books of Dr. Emory Lindquist in the 1940s and 1950s, we all still have questions about the decision of those early Swedish immigrants to settle here in the middle of Kansas, in what was to be known as the Smoky Valley of Kansas. There undoubtedly were other options of territory, state, and land where Lindsborg could have come to being the small city it is today.

During the 1800s a movement of unrest was taking place in Sweden. A Pietistic movement was growing rapidly which had many issues with the Lutheran Church of Sweden, which at this time claimed a vast majority of the citizen as members. These Swedish Pietists were strong-willed Christians with an Evangelistic fervor and belief of worship as they saw fit.

Out of the Pietistic movement came what was known as the läsare (Bible Readers), who met regularly in homes for Bible study, prayer time and fellowship. This met with rigid opposition from the State Church. Even so, Rev. Olof Olsson, serving as Pastor of the Fernebo Lutheran Congregation near Filipstad, was the leader of this movement in the Värmland province of Sweden.

At this point of time in Sweden we can state that Lindsborg was not even a dream, vision or thought of these Swedes who were looking for a better life in a place where they could worship the Lord as they saw fit. Other than wishing for religious freedom, jobs were very difficult to find in Sweden at this time in its history, large families of five to ten children were not uncommon, and the coal and iron industries had not as yet been in operation. A shortage of farmland, and at the same time a population growth, made it hard for farmers to support a family and make a living on the land.

A typical family was that of my grandfather Magnus Carlson's, where he was one of nine children brought up on a small farm near Lungsund in Värmland. He helped his Father farm and was trained as a stone mason and bricklayer, however, land was at a premium for farming, and there was little work available of any kind.

We certainly can empathize with these Swedes as they must have pondered often about their future in Sweden. Yes, they must have been very open to ways to change their lives in the coming years. We wonder today about their dreams and visions of a new country of promise they had just recently been hearing. A land of opportunities. America.

Chapter 2

LAND AGENTS IN SWEDEN

As the läsare movement in Sweden progressed and grew, more unrest occurred among those large families who had children more than ready for the workforce which was negligible in Sweden. Further, stringent rules and regulations seemed to increase, set by the state church which hindered the way many wished to worship in and outside the church. Land agents representing primarily railroad companies in America soon appeared who proclaimed glowing reports of free homestead land in America with an abundance of land to farm in areas where railroads were rapidly being built to the west of the country.

Rev. Olof Olsson encouraged conversations and meetings with these agents which brought excitement about the possibilities of offers which included very reasonable boat rates to the new country thousands of miles away. Rev. Olsson, himself, for a time considered accepting passage and becoming a missionary to the Native Americans of primarily Minnesota.

During this time a Swede teacher and principal in Värmland by the name of C. R. Carlson became an intimate friend of Rev. Olsson as a member of the läsare movement, meeting often with Olsson and groups of Swedes for studying the Bible. Another Carlson, Magnus Carlson, who was employed as stone mason and bricklayer in the area also became a regular member of the läsare group. He was born on June

3, 1838 just a few miles from Lungsund in the province of Värmland on a small farm known as Södra Skällstabacken.

Eventually he was introduced to C. R. Carlson's sister Maria and romance began. They soon agreed to marriage and were married in the Filipstad Lutheran Church by Rev. Olof Olsson on April 17, 1867. These were my grandparents, who had accepted the offer of an Agent, said goodbye to their families and were on the boat heading for America the very next day on April 18. *What a honeymoon*! They arrived in the USA in May long before the Ellis Island Immigration service became the "golden door" for immigrants arriving from Sweden.

An article on Ellis Island states that "over 12 million people were welcomed between 1892 and 1954.

C. R. Carlson and his wife Emilia initially intended to leave Sweden with his sister Maria and brother-in-law Magnus. However, at that time they decided not to because of his handicap, a leg shorter than the other from birth, walking was made difficult for the almost a month-long boat trip to America.

They were soon to change their minds and followed the Magnus Carlsons to the new country as will be noted in a later chapter.

Chapter 3

ARRIVING IN NEW YORK, AND ON WEST TO CHICAGO

Even though a few passengers did not make the almost month-long voyage to New York, as sickness claimed their lives, the newly weds Magnus and Maria Carlson endured the tedious trip.

It was difficult to say goodbye to these new friends who became close and dear friends during the journey on the sea. Further, there were times of doubt as they thought of the large families and friends they left in Sweden.

As planned by land agents the Carlsons soon found passage by rail to Chicago where a large number of earlier Swede immigrants had settled, living with friendly Swedes until finding other temporary living accommodations. Magnus soon found work as a stone mason and bricklayer in the city which was in the midst of a building boom. Although work and pay were satisfactory, the Carlsons disliked the busy schedule of city life, plus having grown up on farms, the possibility of owning their own land further west was very appealing.

There were other Swedes in the Chicago area who often voiced their wishes to investigate homestead land that was being offered in Midwestern states. On the other hand, many of these immigrants established roots in the big city. They were satisfied with the ample opportunities of employment, with some commencing their own businesses.

Chapter 4

LAND AGENTS IN CHICAGO

The First Swedish-American Agricultural Land Company was formed in Chicago on April 17, 1868 according to Dr. Bergin. His earliest book, published in 1909 in Swedish, and later translated by his daughter Ruth Bildt in 1965, states "immigrants in Chicago were being bombarded by numerous land agents," representing many Midwestern states with promises of free homestead land with fertile ground in wide open spaces away from the congestion of cities such as Chicago and New York.

Initially, Magnus Carlson laid temporary claim to 80 acres near Stockholm, Wisconsin. However, he was never able to view the land and later gave up this claim.

It appears the most interest was of land in Wisconsin and Minnesota.

Agents of the railroads were encouraging these Swedish immigrants to look farther west to land that was similar to that of their areas of Sweden. The railroads were anxious to populate the land for protection from Indians who were still living in these Midwestern states. Soon the Land Company commissioned a contingent of their Company to make a journey led by an agent to central Kansas. These men, Anders Olsson, Peter Peterson, A. Jacobson, Magnus Carlson, and L. N. Sandell, were met by John Ferm who had preceded them to view the area. Again, according to Dr. Bergin's writings, these men were all Lutheran immigrants from the province of Värmland in Sweden. Rail fare for them from Chicago to Salina was $10.25.

We can only envision what went through the minds of this group of Swedes when they arrived in what was to be called the Smoky Valley on October 2, 1868. They could see miles and miles of beautiful tall grass, probably from the top of what was later to be named Coronado Heights, and then discovered there were deep creeks and a river winding through the countryside. Further, they must have noticed wisps of smoke from the top of today's Coronado Heights to the west, southwest and northeast where later it was found these were Indian encampments as it was well known this was Indian territory. The largest of these encampments was undoubtedly on Sharp Creek southwest of Lindsborg, given this name due to the fact an earlier Swede attempted to build a home there, but gave up rather quickly due to the presence of Indians.

In the recent past years Indian "digs" have been carried out in these areas where Indians once lived.

Kansas had only become a Territory in 1854 and a State on January 29, 1861. Undoubtedly middle and western Kansas did not become populated earlier due to the scare of Indian raids which will be addressed later. Even so, we must ask, was the land owned by Indians, or was it now owned by the United States Government or by railroads being built through Kansas? Who knows the answer to that question?

These early immigrants moved quickly to erect the Bolaghuset (Company House) just east of Coronado Heights for protection from the upcoming Kansas winter, and also as temporary living quarters for themselves and others who were to follow. The Bolaghuset became the official welcome center for scores of Swedes who began populating the Smoky Valley area.

Chapter 5

SETTLING THE SMOKY VALLEY

Even though the living conditions were tolerable in that early October of 1868, the winter was coming and these hardy Swedes must have been informed somewhat about how severe weather can become here in the heart of this new country. For those who had wives waiting in Chicago correspondence was sent by rail to Salina where they would be met by their husbands with horses and wagons for the journey to their new home in the Valley. Would you agree possibly these women, upon arrival, that they may never have considered divorce? Murder? *Yes*!

These were busy days for these Swedish immigrants, and earliest on their agenda was building the Bolagshuset (Company House) for temporary quarters and for greeting other Swedes who were soon arriving. Homes were being built, crops were being sowed, gardens were planted, homestead land was being claimed. Even though these were tiresome and busy days, time for worship and the building of the first church in the area claimed high priority in the daily lives.

As the Agricultural Company had seen fit to purchase 13,160 acres of land from the Union Pacific Railroad in the area between Coronado Heights and the Smoky Hill River, there was adequate land for all. It is known not all of these early immigrants decided to make permanent homes in the area due to several reasons: The stories of Indian raids, fighting among Indians, the often severe weather, and the fact jobs were still available in Chicago, plus some returned to Sweden.

Magnus Carlson laid claim to homestead land just southeast of Coronado Heights, described as on the south one half of the southeast quarter of section 6 in township 17 south of range 3 west which contains 80 acres. The original deed with this description, signed by President U. S. Grant is today in the possession of his grandson, the author of this work. Early writings differ somewhat on the financing of homestead land. One commentary states one may claim free homestead land of 80 acres with stipulation he lives on and improves the land for five years. Then it is his land. We have read another which states all the homestead land bought at the price of $2.25 per acre. Nevertheless, Magnus Carlson claimed his 80 acres and then at later time purchased an additional 240 acres from the Railroad on section 7 just south of his homestead.

In succeeding years all the homestead land was claimed, bringing more Swedes to discover this new land and new way of existing. These were the toughest of times during the 140 plus years of the Smoky Valley. Those arriving in the Valley had to find places for their families to live, shielded somewhat from the blizzards of winter, and the severe heat of the summer sun. Therefore, we note that dugouts were dug, converted from shallow holes in the ground, or in banks of streams, covered by branches from the few trees in the area.

Today we can note there were at least six dugouts in the area near Lindsborg, and possibly many more, where people spent their time until they could erect a more permanent home for shelter from the ever changing Kansas climate. Further, the few wooded areas were popular places for the immigrants to gather to build some kind of what they called shanties.

During this period Swedes were arriving from several parts of Sweden to settle in the Smoky Valley area. News had spread quickly of available fertile ground in the Valley. Small towns were built in the many farming areas such as Fremount, Smolan, Falun, Salemsborg, Assaria, New Gottland, Marquette, Bridgeport, and Roxbury.

Chapter 6

THE NAMING OF LINDSBORG

Early on, as Swedish immigrants began populating the area, it became apparent the establishment of a town would be possible. A number of those early leaders undoubtedly spent some time in discussing how to approach the naming of the community in what was now becoming a budding and growing settlement. We can only imagine the naming of the city brought much discussion. Could our city have been named New Sweden (at least two small cities in our country today have this name), or Coronado City, Smoky Hill, or Smoky Valley (our high school today is named Smoky Valley).

Certainly it was brought to attention a large number of these early families included Lind in their last names.

Common last names of these first hardy settlers dictated their thinking: Lindberg, Lindquist, Lindahl, Lindgren, Linder, Linde, Linderholm, Lindell and Lindey. "Borg" in Swedish means "city" or "fortified place." It then is easy to understand how this small Swedish community became *Lindsborg*.

However, Lindsborg was not incorporated as a town until July 8,1879 with John A. Swenson as its first Mayor. Mr. Swenson organized the first bank in Lindsborg in 1882, which was privately owned until 1886 when it became a national bank.

The bank building had been built in 1873.

Chapter 7

DUGOUTS IN THE SMOKY VALLEY

Upon arrival in the Smoky Valley in the mid 1860s, immigrants searched for ways and places for some cover from the ever-changing weather of Kansas. Housing was primitive to say the least, with many choosing to dig a dugout in the side of the river bank or small stream, or even in the ground with whatever was available for a roof such as planks and logs covered with grass.

There were no houses or buildings initially in those years from which families could find protection and comfort from the blistering heat of a Kansas summer and the roaring blizzard of snow, wind and ice of the winter months. Later sod houses were relatively easy to build. A special plow was used to break the virgin soil to be used for walls. The floors were usually hard packed soil. Dugouts and sod houses were used for a number of years until more livable homes could be constructed.

We must appreciate these hardy Swedes who struggled against drought, dust, storms, grasshoppers, and the ever-changing ruggedness of nature in this new land. Unrecorded history is the fact a good number of these early Smoky Valley Swedes did not stay long to battle so many climate problems.

A number of infants being born in the Valley did not survive due to these adverse conditions, plus having little or no medical attention available.

Today, remains of at least a half dozen dugouts have been spotted in the Smoky Valley with the belief there were many more. A photo of the Ananias Ebaugh Dugout, located east of Lindsborg, can be found on page 149 in Dr. Bergin's second book on the Smoky Valley. Another on the same page is what is called Smoky Valley Dugout. The Leander Dugout, still in very good condition, is located several miles northeast of Lindsborg. Another photo of a dugout can be found on page 20 in Dr. Bergin's first book of early Pioneer days. Further, a neat stone marker in very good condition is located on the west side of a creek leading into the Smoky Hill River at the south end of Marquette with inscription: DUGOUT SITE, ANDERS SJOGREN, JULY 1869.

Two of the Sjogrens' great-grandchildren live in the Smoky Valley area today. They are Ken Sjogren of Lindsborg, and Marilyn Hendrix of McPherson.

Probably the most well-known dugout in the Valley is the Hoglund Dugout, with information in the next chapter.

Chapter 8

THE HOGLUND DUGOUT

The story of the Hoglund Dugout is of an amazing and unique early Smoky Valley family, the Gustaf Hoglund family, who lived just west of the city limits of Lindsborg, Kansas.

Arriving in the fall of 1868, Gustaf was one of the first to immigrate from the Värmland province, Sweden, to Kansas, where he pioneered the Smoky Valley of this state, and settled on acreage, part of which was Homestead land.

With no accommodations for living available, he selected an area with a grove of trees near a creek on the west side of his new property and proceeded to dig a dugout to serve as some protection against the ever-changing Kansas climate.

The Dugout today is now a historical site, which marks the place of an early Scandinavian home, with the Smoky Valley Historical Association being responsible for the preservation and maintenance of the site. To view the Dugout today, one's imagination can yield all kinds of difficult possibilities of the living conditions of early settlers.

Gustaf Hoglund was born on July 18, 1841 in Fernebo (Persberg) in the province of Värmland, Sweden. Bethany Lutheran church in Lindsborg shows records that Mr. Hoglund was received as a member of the church on March 18, 1872.

Maria Mathilda Olsson Hoglund was born in Fernebo, Sweden on September 20, 1846 and arrived with her parents in the Smoky Valley in 1868, and was received as a member of the church on September 1, 1869. On January 8, 1871 the Hoglunds were married in Bethany Lutheran Church by Rev. Olof Olsson, having previously served the same parish in Persberg, Värmland, Pastor Olsson was undoubtedly well acquainted with the couple.

The Hoglunds immigrated to America for the same reasons as most of the Swedish emigrants, the promise of land on which to make a living, religious freedom to worship as they saw fit, as well as large families in Sweden making employment scarce in the old country.

According to reports from family members of the early Smoky Valley immigrants the Dugout constructed by Gustaf Hoglund was where they had their first two children, Gustaf born on February 13, 1872 and Selma on August 19, 1873. During this time the Hoglunds were not only busy farming, but also in erecting a small shanty-like building on the creek bank near their Dugout which would serve as their second home in the Valley for several years. During these years their third and fourth children were born; Emil on March 19, 1875 and Lydia on June 16, 1877. Also during these busy years the Hoglunds were building a large two-story, five-bedroom home in the middle of their acreage with a beautiful wraparound porch, a large kitchen, and family living room area.

Some time in the late 1870s the Hoglund family moved into this home where they proceeded to add to their growing family with four more children being born: Elizabeth on July 18, 1879, Gustaf Simon on April 2, 1884, Anna Olivia on May 26, 1886 and Alma Sophia on May 19, 1888. Bethany Lutheran Church records show that all eight children were baptized with their baptismal dates. There have been reports a ninth child had been born, however, there are no recorded records of this birth which was probably due to death in childbirth.

Having eight children on the Prairie of Central Kansas was not at all unusual in those early days of the Smoky Valley. Now what seems quite unusual is that none of the eight Hoglund children ever married.

Further, the Hoglunds proved to be a healthy family tolerating the severe Kansas very cold winters and very hot summers rather well. In spite of the fact their first child died at the age of six months, the others lived long past life expectancy to the ages of 74, 86, 93, 81, 63, and 87. In contrast, one family located a little over a mile from the Hoglund farm also had eight children. However, the infant virus, so prevalent in 1870s and 1880s took its toll, four deaths occurring from two weeks old to one year, with the other four living to the ages of 19, 44, 83, and 84. I am referring to the children of my paternal grandparents, pioneers Magnus and Maria Carlson. The names of their nineteen-year-old daughter and four infant sons and daughters are listed on the same tombstone at the Rose Hill Cemetery located a few miles north of Lindsborg.

As the family grew, the Hoglund farming operation also grew with additional land purchased, and the erection of a large barn and milk shed located near their home. According to stories from early-day Swedes, the Hoglunds were a tight knit family keeping pretty much to themselves, all working long hours farming the land, tending an extraordinary and large garden. The family was faithful in attending Sunday morning worship in Bethany Lutheran Church where for many years Mr. Hoglund served as a trustee. Long time members of the church have mentioned that at the end of each year, when church funds were running low, the Hoglunds were always ready to contribute generously.

No one today could attest to the Hoglund children attending school in Lindsborg, or any of the country schools in the area, although there was one about two miles northwest of their home. Possibly they were some of the first home-schooled children in the Valley. It is known the Father was opposed to higher education, according to the Attorney and Executor of their wills.

On most Saturday mornings in the thirties and forties, as the writer of this story can remember, the Hoglund four-door Model T traveled, with doors flapping in the wind, on the main road into town on West Lincoln Street, heading for the business district to sell eggs and some garden supplies, while picking up groceries for the coming week. For many years West Lincoln Street, a mixture of dirt and sand, served as the play ground for a number of games, with children appreciating the slow "putt putt" of the Hoglund Model T not raising expected dust as was usually true of other vehicles.

Following the deaths of Mr. and Mrs. Hoglund, the family of eight continued their Saturday morning shopping trips to town in the way they were taught.

Gustaf Hoglund passed away on June 14, 1922 at the age of 81, and was preceded in death by Maria Hoglund on February 8, 1920 at the age of 74. The children of the Hoglunds continued their successful farming operation for many years.

The family estate had been placed in the trust of the President of the Farmers State Bank in Lindsborg, Mr. C. A. Abercrombie. Following the death of Alma Sophia, at the age of 87, on June 22, 1975, the Hoglund estate was divided between Bethany Lutheran Church, Bethany Home, and the Lindsborg Hospital, with the church receiving one half of the estate (approximately $300,000) and Bethany Home and the Lindsborg Hospital receiving one quarter, (approximately $150,000). The hospital had been home for Alma Sophia for the final years of her life. The church then gave $100,000 of their share to Bethany Home to assist in building a new wing, named the Hoglund wing.

Undoubtedly, there are many other stories and tales to be told about the Gustaf Hoglund family who lived just west of Lindsborg. Hopefully, through this study of this unique and amazing early Lindsborg family, we have been able to preserve some history of Lindsborg from its earliest days. Unfortunately, there are no Hoglund family members in the community to add to their legacy today.

After all: *history not recorded, is perhaps history lost.*

Chapter 9

AN EARLY LINDSBORG COMMUNITY LEADER

One of those very early community leaders of Lindsborg was a man by the name of C. R. Carlson, noted a number of times as a very active community business leader, in the books of Dr. Alfred Bergin and Dr. Emory Lindquist as well as Alf Brorson of Torsby, Sweden. He was born on a farm in the province of Värmland, Sweden.

C. R. Carlson was a member of the läsare group that had been meeting regularly in Sweden with Rev. Olof Olsson to read and study the Bible. C. R. was a brother-in-law of Magnus Carlson who preceded him here in the Smoky Valley. C. R. and Magnus had become intimate friends of Rev. Olsson while Pastor Olsson was serving the Fernebo congregation, prior to his call to the Sunnemo Church. Carlson was serving as the Principal and Teacher in the area.

Upon Magnus Carlson's arrival in the Smoky Valley, he soon sent a letter to his brother-in-law C. R. Carlson urging him and his wife Emilia to join them in this new-found country, which they did late in December of 1868.

We would point out here in Mr. Brorson's writings he emphasizes, "that contrary to what many thought, these Swedish immigrants coming to America were not the very poor or indigent, but had some financial means to assist in settling in this new country, and the poor in Sweden could not afford the trip over, and the rich were too well-off financially to consider such a move."

The early writers of the history of Lindsborg all point to the fact C. R. Carlson possessed strong leadership abilities. His lameness, being born with one leg much shorter than the other, and his piety, plus his education, no doubt impressed people in the area as they were settling into this new way of life.

Dr. Bergin, in his book *Smoky Valley People in the After Years*, states "when C. R. Carlson arrived in the Smoky Valley he gathered people around God's word on Sundays as well as at other times." Further, he talked to some of his countrymen about the need for calling a Pastor, resulting in his writing a letter back to Sweden to his good friend Rev. Olof Olsson, who accepted the "call," and arrived with his family at Midsummer 1869.

A small church was hastily constructed in section 6 on land owned by Magnus Carlson, who served as the Foreman on the project. It was located on a hill in the middle of the section with plans to build a city around the church. Today a large concrete pillar marks the spot of this first church, which can be viewed from all four corners of the section. C. R. Carlson, whose influence must have been strong, changed the site of the town to the north side of what was to be named the Smoky Hill river in section 17, and where a railroad was being built.

Before Rev. Olsson arrived, C. R. Carlson served as Lay Pastor leading worship services on Sundays in his home and others being built in the area, also baptizing, marrying and conducting burial rites.

As told by Dr. Lindquist in his book, *Smoky Valley People*, "in November, 1869, C. R. Carlson, John Ferm and A. Jacobson laid out the town site in the middle of section 17.

In the absence of surveying instruments, they used a square, a tape measure and guesswork."

Old Timers in the community loved to relate stories about the effort of these three gentlemen. One can notice a pronounced bend today that Main Street takes near Bethany Lutheran Church. This was attributed to the fact C. R. had one leg shorter than the other, or as others claimed, as the gentlemen sited from north to south, the mid-center of Lindsborg was still pasture land where cows were grazing; unfortunately the men had settled on one hungry cow which kept moving as she grazed. Stranger and more embellished stories of the laying out of Main Street have sensibly passed on.

In 1871, C. R. Carlson commenced a long and successful career as a business man, along with his good friend Dan Johnson. Initially they built a small wood frame store on the northeast comer of Main and Lincoln Street in the very center of the town. This building, known as the "Ark', was used as their general store with the second floor as the community's first school, taught by C. R. Carlson. Soon they sold this property to J. O. Sundstrom and then built a larger store on the southwest corner of this intersection. This property is now the Swisher Firestone store, owned and operated by Dwight Swisher.

J. O. Sundstrom then built what still is the largest Downtown brick building in Lindsborg on the north-east corner of Main and Lincoln, which dates back to 1879. The building has had a number of uses and has been owned by the city for the past eight years. Plans are for major renovations to the property by the city which will be covered in the *Lindsborg Now* section of this writing.

C. R. Carlson held many positions in the community, including City Council and for a time as Postmaster. With some certainly, C. R. Carlson and his wife Emilia (Emile) would surely be remembered as some of the most active citizens of early Lindsborg.

Would it not be an exciting venture to take the C. R. Carlsons on a tour of our fine city today?

Chapter 10

REV. OLOF OLSSON, FOUNDER OF LINDSBORG

Soon after C. R. Carlson's arrival in the Smoky Valley, he sent a letter to Rev. Olof Olsson that he had been authorized to send him a "call" to come to America and become the Pastor of this new settlement.

Dr. Bergin and again Dr. Lindquist relate that Olsson initially was not able to persuade his close friend C. R. not to immigrate to America, but had finally said to him, "alright, go in the name of the Lord, and if you find a place in America where God's children may dwell in peace and worship God at their hearts dictate, write to me and I will come."

The people among whom Dr. Olsson was to work had dreamed of a flawless and perfect congregation under his leadership and guidance. They were all Pietists, Lutheran by confession, and opposed to the state church of Sweden. They believed sincerely in freedom and were eager for the separation of church and state. Further, it was evident Dr. Olsson was not pleased with the conditions in the state church of Sweden and was not well-liked by some of his enemies in the state church.

The "call" was sent to Olsson sometime in December. Olsson accepted and arrived in the summer of 1869. Olsson had gathered 250 Swedes who left Sweden together, headed for America. Some writings state that all arrived in the Smoky Valley that summer. Others say eighty families, while in other places we read 124 arrived in the Valley, which seems more likely, with some staying in Chicago where there was ample employment, and others wound up in Bucklin, Missouri. Interesting to note, those who went to Bucklin because of promise of work in the coal industry and railroads being built, did not stay long, with most moving on to northern Kansas settling the communities of Scandia, Kackley, and Courtland. Still others had heard of Indian raids and even massacres in the state of Kansas plus the fact they would be initially living in very primitive conditions.

Nevertheless, Dr. Olsson became the leader and recognized founder of the community of Lindsborg. Dr. Lindquist emphasized in his writings that "Olsson's record of achievement in the seven years between 1869 and 1876 is remarkable. Pastor of a large and growing congregation, missionary, county superintendent of schools, a member of the Kansas House of Representatives, writer, editor, musician, choir director and friend of people. Olof Olsson gave himself unsparingly in the cause that was Lindsborg."

Further, the changing and sometimes severe Kansas weather did not deter Pastor Olsson from looking after the needs of his people as he made his way around the Smoky Valley, whether by walking or horseback.

There are reams of stories that could be related about Dr. Olsson's energetic leadership in the founding of Lindsborg and his many contributions during his rather short stay here. For those interested, they may search the writings of Dr. Bergin, Dr. Lindquist, Alf Brorson, A. John Pearson and others for more about his life here in Lindsborg.

Dr. Olof Olsson, spiritual founder of Lindsborg, represents *Lindsborg Then* in those late 1860s and early 1870s.

Chapter 11

CHURCH DIVISION AND CONTROVERSY

A few years after the first church was erected in section 7, a split occurred due to a number of controversies, not the least of which was the issue of atonement. A number of differing opinions led to a deep split among close friends who were active members of the Church of Sweden, as well as disagreement of the real meaning of atonement.

Following much study and conversations at various times, the writer can express some frustration as to how these dedicated early Christian settlers could become so upset regarding the atonement issue. Today we find the issue of atonement to be of a minor issue as it relates to salvation and the belief in Jesus as our Saviour and Lord, for He has atoned for all of our sins on the cross at Calvary. It is the acceptance of Jesus as our Saviour that leads us to a heavenly home when our days are over here on earth.

It is understandable there are those who will take issue with this particular paragraph.

It would appear a number of other disagreements were included in the split. The reason for immigrating for some was church freedom, a more informal structure of worship, strong personalities, strict rules of Rev. Olof Olsson, and his insistence on belonging to the Augustana Lutheran Synod of America. Many expressed the fear of once again becoming oppressed in their worship with hard fast rules as they experienced with the state church of Sweden. Further, many yearned for a more informal worship with less liturgy involved in their Sunday services.

There were those who were not pleased by the admission of Dr. Olsson and the congregation into the Augustana Synod which occurred at a meeting in Andover, Illinois in 1870. There was much grumbling among the people who opposed this move. Dr. Olsson answered them by stating that it was not good to exist as an individual congregation, but that it was necessary to belong to some group or communion, as he felt the Augustana Synod was the best and most logical.

A few of the immigrants had organized Bible Studies and Prayer Meetings in various homes in the absence at times of Rev. Olsson, who felt threatened by the possibilities of members slipping away from what he had envisioned in Sweden, that of a "pure" church. Rev. Olsson frowned on the practice of inviting travelling missionaries into members' homes and welcoming them to speak in their church.

Another area of contention was the practice of baptism and the necessity of a conversion, or recommitment experience at the age of accountability. Friendships were weakened and families were split over these spiritual issues that arose among church members. Hot discussions in the stores and on the streets of Lindsborg were very common.

During this time a new church had been built in Lindsborg, on North Main Street, and was soon ready for worship services. It was about this time the division occurred within the Bethany Lutheran membership.

Dr. Lindquist, in *Smoky Valley People*, states "between 1874–1876 forty-two members either withdrew membership or were excommunicated by Rev. Olsson from the pulpit on a Sunday morning." Ten of the twelve charter council members left the church.

The Swedish Evangelical Mission Covenant Church was established in Sweden in 1878. Most of those who left Bethany Lutheran Church quickly joined the new Swedish Mission Church which had been built in the Rose Hill area north of Lindsborg, and later on the corner of Lincoln and Washington in Lindsborg.

In addressing the church split over spiritual practices and beliefs, it must be emphasized that the healing began to occur slowly in the late 1870s. Old friends once again spoke to each other, transacted business with each other, bringing unity and forgiveness among these hardy, strong-willed and hard-working Swedes. It has been said, if it had not been for the fact these settlers from Sweden were strong in opinions, and were people who were determined to seek the Scripture, they would never have been successful in the new country over five thousand miles from their homeland.

Rev. Olsson, in poor health, left Lindsborg in 1876 taking a leave of absence. He never again served as Pastor of Bethany Lutheran Church. He and his family frequently returned to the Smoky Valley where they were warmly received. Quoting again from Dr. Lindquist's writings, "Rev. Olsson, upon his return in 1888 for Holy Week, was asked to preach in the Swedish Mission Covenant Church on Palm Sunday evening where he was received with hugs, wide smiles, and yes, tears of reconciliation."

Throughout the late 1800s and even up through the 1930s and 1940s, some tension seemed to be continued between the Lutherans and the Covenant people. Very few religious functions took place in Lindsborg including all churches in town. One major break though commenced in the mid-1920s with elementary students attending the church of their choice for Wednesday released morning sessions of the Bible.

Some years later there was additional cooperation among all local churches when third and fourth grade students met on Wednesdays in the Covenant Church and the fifth and sixth grade students in Bethany Lutheran Church with teachers from all local churches. These became optional to all students some time later, but even so, today around two thirds of these students take advantage of these released time Bible sessions.

During the early to mid-1900s it seemed there was almost an unwritten "tabu" for a Lutheran boy to date a Covenant girl, or a Covenant boy to date a Lutheran girl. There seemed to be some sort of suspicion.

One family of three brothers sort of broke the ice between the churches in the 1940s as the oldest Covenant boy commenced dating a Messiah Lutheran girl which became the subject of conversation. A few years later his brother started dating another Messiah Lutheran girl. This brought questions and some light rumblings among a number of both Lutheran and Covenant members.

When the youngest brother became involved dating still another Messiah Lutheran girl the Father of the boys would only smile when questioned, saying nothing. However, he was encountered one day by several men from his church with "Why do all your sons date those Lutheran girls and not our Covenant girls?" Undoubtedly tired of all the questioning the Father's reply was simply, "I will tell you why. It is because those Lutheran girls are so much prettier than our Covenant girls." Case closed.

And yes, all three Covenant boys married their Lutheran girlfriends.

Chapter 12

INDIANS IN THE SMOKY VALLEY

In his book, *The Smoky Valley in the After Years,* we quote Dr. Bergin as follows, "a more restless and wild territory than Kansas was not to be found during the 1830s through the 1850s, in the whole country. Indian tribes were at war with each other and bloodshed was a daily occurrence."

In the mid-1860s a few hardy Swedes had attempted to settle in the Smoky Valley area. However, their stay in the Valley was short-lived due to stories of Indian raids and massacres. Isaac Sharp was one of these who settled long enough to build a small log cabin for not only his home, but to serve as a Trading Post.

Dr. Lindquist, in his book *Smoky Valley People,* states an interesting fact that Mr. Sharp was probably the first white person to settle in the area, but due to the many Indians in the area, he soon took up residence in Council Grove, Kansas area, where he became an active politician and democratic candidate for governor of Kansas in 1870.

Even though the first covered wagons crossed Kansas on the Santa Fe Trail in the early and mid-1800s, it took many years for settlers to choose mid-Kansas land as their homes. This was probably due to the fact the territory was held by Osage, Pawnee and Paduca Indian tribes.

Alan Lindfors and Eleanor Burnison in their book on the History of Marquette, located just west of Lindsborg, state the following. "Indians were a constant worry for early settlers. Although the Indians would often beg and steal and frighten women, there was actually little harm done. Most of the Indians in this vicinity were Kaw, inclined to laziness, begging and petty thievery, but on the whole good-natured and friendly. But the early settlers, and especially the Swedes, weren't aware of this. They were terrified because of rumors and incidents."

Dr. Bergin, in his book *Pioneer Swedish American Culture*, states "Sam Shields, as early as the fall of 1866 established a business where trade was carried on briefly with Indians who traded buffalo hides etc, for the necessities of life. Shields closed his business just prior to the arrival of the representatives of the First Swedish-American Agricultural Company in the late 1860s."

Bergin again relates an interesting story about the Indians in the Smoky Valley. "In the year 1873, there was a tribe of Indians which camped seven miles northwest of Marquette. These Indians were quite friendly, but would often annoy the old settlers begging food and tobacco. One day five Indians came to a farm house for the purpose of begging food. The lady of the house gave them bread she had just baked. While she was talking to them one Indian sneaked around to another door, entered the house, and concealed all the bread under his blanket. When the lady went to wrap the bread she found it was all gone."

Further Dr. Lindquist, in *Smoky Valley People*, relates the following: "Swedes in the Smoky Valley experienced no serious difficulty with the Indians. Bands of Indians crossed the Valley from time to time, but there was no armed conflict with them. They came to dwellings begging for food and other items. Occasionally there was petty thievery. The settlers often recounted that when they were butchering, it was quite likely that Indians would appear."

The only recorded strife with Indians involving Lindsborg residents, occurred in May, 1869. P. M. Elmquist and Peter Johnson were seeking Elmquist's father and brother who had settled northwest of Salina. They were reunited when on a Sunday afternoon a band of Indians attacked them in their dugout. The Swedes escaped injury, but in the battle two Indians were killed. The raid was part of the attack by Sioux Indians along Spilman Creek in Lincoln County, where thirteen settlers were killed. Interesting to note, Lindsborg resident Larry Elmquist is a great grandson of P. M. Elmquist who was a farmer and carpenter northwest of Lindsborg. He had immigrated from Växjö in Central Sweden in the late 1860s.

Ken Sjogren, also of Lindsborg, in his story on the Sjogren Family and their settlement in the Marquette area, relates an interesting story of family members "who for the first time while they lived in their dugout, some boys saw the Indians coming, so they warned the women and children. The men were gone, so the children hid under beds and tables. One of the Indians came to the door and Mrs. Hanson, who was a little braver than the others, gave the Indians some bread and meat."

On another occasion, some time later, "the Sjogrens and the Hedbergs were on their way home from services at the Fremont Lutheran Church and met a band of Indians. The greeting was 'how' or 'ha' and by raising their right hands. The Indians in the vicinity were inclined to laziness, begging and petty thievery. The Kaw Indians of the time were good-natured and friendly. For protection from the Indians, the government had issued each family with a musket and some ammunition."

While there was no record of conflict by the Swede settlers with the Indians who were still living in the Smoky Valley, precautions were taken in the event of danger from the roving bands of Indian hunters. In June 1869, according to Dr. Lindquist, "members of the Swedish-American Agricultural Company of Chicago were authorized expenditures for forty-seven rifles and six pistols." These were issued to settlers in the Smoky Valley.

Our father, Paul Carlson, regaled his children and later his grandchildren with stories about Indians who lived a few miles away from his home in section 6 which was halfway between Coronado Heights and the city of Lindsborg. In the 1880s, and early 1990s, on occasion Indians would ride their horses into the farm yards of the Swedes, especially when butchering of hogs and beef was taking place. These were times when neighbors would gather to share in the work.

It was said the Indians could smell the scent of butchering from miles away. Further, it was thought the Indians made broth and soup from the tails and heads of the animals. They would watch from their horses the butchering process and point to the tails and heads, and even the hoofs of the animals, making known their wishes. Our Dad said his father Magnus Carlson, was very generous to the Indians as he told his sons, "we certainly want to keep them happy."

The Indians would make signs of thanks for the animal parts and ride off on their horses. A few times they would take time to stop and admire the horses the Carlsons kept in and near their barn. At first there was concern the Indians some day would come and steal horses. Dad said "this never happened" which speaks well for the mutual admiration and respect the Indians and the settlers had for each other.

A favorite story, which his children, and later his grandchildren, begged often for Dad to tell was when several Indians came riding on their ponies to the farm house one day, and motioned to Grandmother Carlson that they were hungry. Magnus and a neighbor had gone by horse and buggy to Salina for an overnight trip for supplies. Grandma Carlson and our Dad Paul, who was about five years old and Nathaniel who was two years older took the Indians to the basement of the house where meat was salted and stored along with canned food. One tough-looking Indian took a large knife while holding Nathaniel and placed the knife at his throat in a menacing manner.

Nathaniel, scared to death, did not move, while Grandma Carlson gesturing to the Indians to take all the meat and canned goods they wanted, but to leave Nathaniel alone.

Possibly the Indians had miscalculated, and thought it must be time to butcher, or simply were hungry. The big Indian was only kidding and with a smile patted Nathaniel on the back as he put his knife away. They would then only accept a few pieces of meat, mounted their horses and rode off with smiles and waves for which Grandma Carlson was very relieved. Needless to say, the Indians spoke only their language and Dad's family spoke only Swedish. We might add here, that Dad and his brothers and sisters did not know any English until the were enrolled in the English-speaking country school located a few miles from their home.

Our Father said in the early 1890s all the Indians had moved on and had disappeared from the Smoky Valley. He had no idea what happened to them. Others have said their last village in the Smoky Valley was by Paint Creek, located several miles southwest of Lindsborg. A number of successful Indian "digs" have been conducted in the Paint Creek area during the past few years.

Dr. Lindquist, in his book *Smoky Valley People*, states the following, "the attacks by Indians along Sharp Creek in 1867 and nearby areas in 1869 led to the organization of a Home Protection Company in the Smoky Valley during the later years. Major L. N. Holmberg was placed in command.

A sod fort was built southeast of Marquette for this purpose.

There were no attacks or Indian scares after this period.

History not recorded, is perhaps history lost.

Chapter 13

ANOTHER EARLY SMOKY VALLEY LEADER, MAGNUS CARLSON

In the fall of 1868 the First Swedish-American Agricultural Company of Chicago sent a group of six of its members to the Smoky Valley in the heart of Kansas to survey the unbroken land available for homesteading.

Magnus Carlson was one of these men, which led to the settling of the Valley. Some facts of his life are pertinent to point out why he chose to immigrate to this strange new country from a rather comfortable life in Sweden.

Born on a small farm on July 3, 1838 near Lungsund in the province of Värmland, Sweden, he was one of nine children of Karl Magnus Carlson. While a teenager he was trained as a stone mason and bricklayer, a trade that was to become valuable in his years in the Smoky Valley of Kansas. After being introduced to the läsare movement in Värmland, and to Rev. Olof Olsson, Magnus and Maria were married on April 17, 1867 by Rev. Olsson in the Filipstad Lutheran Church, and left on a boat for America on the very next day, April 18. Maria was a sister of well-known Swede C. R. Carlson, a Teacher and Principal when Rev. Olsson was serving the Fernebo Lutheran congregation.

After spending almost a year in Chicago, Magnus and several other Swedes formed the First Swedish-American Agricultural Company, and he was part of a group of men from the Company who were convinced by a land agent that they should go to mid-Kansas to view the territory which only recently became officially the state of Kansas. Magnus had already laid claim to 80 acres of Homestead land in Wisconsin. However, he was still anxious to see land further west in this new country, and according to family history he never saw the land in Wisconsin.

The group arrived on October 2, 1868 and were immediately impressed with what was to become known as the Smoky Valley of Kansas. They saw acres and acres of grassland for miles and miles, and spotted a high hill, which was later named Coronado Heights, from which the view was even more stunning. Soon a river was spotted winding through the Valley and the soil seemed fertile. Of course the river was soon named the Smoky Hill River.

The Swedish-American Land Company then purchased 13,160 acres from the Union Pacific Railroad. The railroads were commencing to be laid through the area to the west and railroad officials felt it was important to inhabit the land to discourage Indian pillage of trains headed west. It was soon discovered what they had been told, that Kansas had several dozen Indian tribes inhabiting the area, including land just west of Coronado Heights, south-west and north-east of the present city of Lindsborg.

Magnus claimed 80 acres of Homestead land in section 6 located halfway between Coronado Heights and the Smoky Hill River. He soon also purchased 240 acres in section 7 just north of section 6, from the railroad. We can note here, one of his grandsons has the original Homestead Certificate of the 80 acres, signed by President U. S. Grant. The certificate hangs in his home, just under a painting by local artist Maleta Forsberg of the first stone house in the Valley built on the Homestead acreage by Magnus Carlson.

Further, according to Dr. Alfred Bergin, Carlson was the foreman on the first church in the Smoky Valley which was built on his land in section 7, as well as the first home for Rev. Olof Olsson, constructed just west of the Carlson home on section 6 one mile south of Coronado Heights.

A letter back to Sweden to the C. R. Carlsons brought them to America and the Smoky Valley in late 1868. As has been written previously, C. R. Carlson became the leader of the immigrants until the arrival of Rev. Olof Olsson in the early summer of the following year to become the spiritual and community leader and the prime founder of the city of Lindsborg.

Magnus continued for years as a farmer, stone mason and bricklayer in the Smoky Valley. He built the C. R. home on the corner of Lincoln and Washington in Lindsborg in 1887, now known as the Christians Funeral Home. He served as the foreman of bricklayers when Old Main was built on the campus of Bethany College in the late 1880s.

Magnus and Maria had nine children. Due to a virus raging throughout the Smoky Valley, tough living conditions, and lack of medical attention in those early days, their first four children died from two weeks to twenty-one months. The remaining five children lived to ripe old ages, with only one living out his life with his wife Agnes here in Lindsborg. The Paul Carlsons had five children, the youngest of whom is the writer of this history.

* * *

Apologies are in order for this chapter of Lindsborg history. A delicate way could not be found to relate local history without including the happenings in the life of family members. However, it is important to history, to record history before it is lost to time forever.

Chapter 14

DR. ALFRED BERGIN

The community of Lindsborg owes a deep appreciation to Dr. Alfred Bergin, long-time Pastor of Bethany Lutheran Church, for his part in researching and preserving the history of Lindsborg and the Smoky Valley. If it had not been for his authoring the two earliest books of early history of this small town settled by Swedish immigrants, much history would be gone forever.

Dr. Bergin's books can be read, and read again and again, as one becomes more and more interested in the facts, people, places and times related to the late 1860s into the 1900s.

In early 1904 members of Bethany Lutheran Church and the community received with deep grief the news that Dr. Carl Swensson had died. Dr. Swensson, who had succeeded Dr. Olof Olsson, left a positive impact on the church and community during his brief time in Lindsborg. Members wondered who would take Dr. Swensson's place.

Pastor Erland Anderson reports that at a meeting on June 21, 1904 the congregation issued a call to the Pastor of the Swedish Evangelical Lutheran congregation in Cambridge, Minnesota, Dr. of Philosophy Alfred Bergin. It was felt by both the congregation and Dr. Bergin that it was the will of God for him to be called to Bethany Lutheran Church here in Lindsborg.

It was soon found Dr. Bergin was a prolific writer and was to become the first to publish books regarding life in the Smoky Valley. Today, well over a hundred years later, Dr. Bergin's writings still contain the information used as we look back on the history of this community.

Dr. Bergin was remembered for his rather thunderous voice as he commenced each Sunday morning worship service with a resounding "Helig, Helig, Helig" (Holy, Holy, Holy). Further his attention to detail was an inspiration to all who knew him. It was said he ruled the church with an iron hand.

In 1908 English-speaking persons had moved into the community, particularly staff members at Bethany College, which had commenced operation in 1881. All worship services were being conducted in Swedish. A group requested a meeting with Dr. Bergin to propose an English-speaking Lutheran Church in the community. Local "lore" tells us when he was asked if he or God would have any problem with this happening, it was said his reply was, after great thought: "No, I won't, but God may."

Shortly after, the Messiah Lutheran Church was organized as an English-speaking congregation with services held in the Chapel of Bethany College.

Bethany Home was built and opened in November of 1911 with Dr. Bergin as President of the Home's board of directors, a position he held for many years. The first eleven elderly residents moved into the home in late 1911. However, the home was constructed for almost twenty residents. It was decided to allow a number of orphan children to live in the home, which obviously meant much activity and noise, and from the pulpit one Sunday morning, Dr. Bergin announced "they are trying to have children in Bethany Home, and it's not working." Was this some Bergin humor, was it a "gaffe" or was it just the truth?

We can not conclude this appreciation for Dr. Bergin's contributions to our community without also including writers Dr. Emory Lindquist, Alf Brorson and A. John Pearson in our appreciation for their many gifts of information concerning the preservation of early history of Lindsborg. We again are reminded: History not recorded, is perhaps history lost.

Chapter 15

ELLIS ISLAND

Ellis Island, New York has a magic name for many immigrants arriving on American soil in the 1890s up until around the 1950s. The American Profile Magazine tells us that Ellis Island was the "golden door" for over twenty-five million people from scores of European countries who fled to America for work, or from political and religious oppression.

Although Ellis Island was not open in the years when the immigrants were coming to the Smoky Valley of Kansas, many had relatives who joined them years later here in Lindsborg. Ellis Island did not open its doors until 1892 when it represented a symbol of welcome and arrival and opportunities. These immigrants were well inspected by officials who wanted them coming over ready, willing and able to work.

It was reported in the above-mentioned magazine that "string-tied bundles, suitcases, and trunks of personal belongings came with the immigrants plus mementos from their faraway homes."

Mrs. Agda Jacobson came to Lindsborg from her home in Kansas City in the 1980s to become a resident in the Bethany Home Cottages where she lived for a number of years. Mrs. Jacobson, a native of Sweden, had owned and operated a Scandinavian gift shop in Kansas City for many years. Her story of coming through Ellis Island from her childhood home in Sweden was most interesting. It became more interesting as she related she had contributed her trunk to Ellis Island when she moved to Lindsborg, and that it had her name in large black letters on a side.

A few years later when my wife and I were traveling on a bus tour of the East, Ellis Island was of interest, knowing Mrs. Jacobson made her entry into the United States here. The Island has information on over twenty-five million immigrants from 1892 to 1924 listed on the walls of the museum's American Family Immigration History Center. Not only did we find the name of Agda Jacobson, which jived with the year she arrived, but also, by chance, we viewed her trunk with her name, piled with a huge group of trunks. Her name could also be found online on a computer.

The early Smoky Valley Swedish immigrants to America from the 1860s to 1891 missed the Ellis Island experience of the exceptional warm welcome given later to those who followed. Undoubtedly these Swedes made their way to the Midwest thanks to family members who preceded them or by land agents who were still extolling the virtues of available work and land in center of the United States.

Chapter 16

COOPERATIVE FARMING IN THE SMOKY VALLEY

The agricultural community of the Scandinavian farmers who settled in the Smoky Valley worked closely together during times of threshing and whenever a neighbor needed assistance with field work.

Farming experience in Sweden by almost all of the immigrants became beneficial as they commenced preparing the ground for crops. Each farm family planted large gardens and milked their cows, while the men and older boys spent long hours in farming their land, but also were employed as laborers in the construction of homes, buildings and roads in the Valley.

Mr. Elmer Lindholm, a delightful long-time resident of Bethany Home in Lindsborg, who passed away a number of years ago at the age of 102, related stories of those past years when neighbors from miles around would join with what he called "threshing bees."

Wives and daughters who joined in these efforts would provide some of the best meals Elmer had ever tasted. These frequent workdays provided opportunities for families to become better acquainted. The Lindholm homestead was located several miles northwest of Lindsborg. Elmer was one of the last who could share firsthand stories of those early Smoky Valley days.

Even though Elmer Lindholm and his family were all strong Baptists, he said with a twinkle in his eye, "we all got along with all those Lutherans, and even the Covenanters, when it came to working with one another. We would help them with their work, and they would help us with ours."

Further, Mr. Lindholm loved to relate stories of neighboring farmers who would gather on one farm once or twice each year to share in the tedious task of butchering their animals. He witnessed to the fact Indians would often show up during these butchering days begging for parts of the animals.

A World War I veteran, having served on the front lines of battle in Europe, his stories of battle field experiences were priceless and should have been preserved.

Chapter 17

ENTERTAINMENT FOR PIONEERS IN THE 1860s

Long workdays, sunup until sundown, six days each week by these early immigrants in the Smoky Valley with only Sunday as a breaktime, one has to wonder that surely they must have spent some time away from hard labor to enjoy the clean air and sites of the Valley.

There were no radios, televisions, cars, electricity, gas, movies, computers, concerts, programs, McDonalds, Pizza Huts, no place like Presser Hall on the campus of Bethany College, and all other what they would call "niceties," which we take for granted today in Lindsborg in the *Now*!

According to Dr. Lindquist, in his book *Smoky Valley People*, "reports of the Bethany Lutheran Church include almost annual warnings about the evils of dancing and the action by deacons to maintain discipline at that point."

Further, it appeared some of the residents of Lindsborg in pioneer days enjoyed social dancing on the sly.

Celebrations of birthdays and anniversaries were important to Swedes in the old country and those continued in the Smoky Valley, which proved to be their time of fellowship and entertainment. The pious spirit of these immigrants discouraged the use of alcohol or tobacco.

Families lived in close quarters in small dugouts and sod houses eating their meals, praying and studying together. Families grew rapidly with some having as many as six to thirteen children. Dare we say, tongue-in-cheek, "that much time must have been spent in bedrooms." We do know from early writings that Sundays were sacred with all who were able attending church worship, coming from all directions with horse and buggy and farm wagons.

With most having large families it would be safe to say children in each family could find ways to entertain each other. There was a way to entertain the very young with the following Swedish rhyme while bouncing them on a knee, which usually brought giggles and expressions of delight as follows:

Rida, Rida, Ranka
Hästen heter Blanca
Vatt skall du rida
Till en liten piga
Vad skall hon heta
Anna Margareta
Den tjocka och feta

Dr. Lindquist in his book *Smoky Valley People* states "the text of this rhyme is not particularly significant, but the singing and the action furnished entertainment for children and adults." This tradition of entertainment for the young has been carried on through the years with those of Swedish descent in our community and in other locations of Swedes.

Chapter 18

CLOSE KNIT FAMILIES

The immigrant families, by and large were close knit, working, eating, praying, worshipping together. All members of the family rose early each morning with chores to carry out before sitting down to an ample breakfast prepared by the women of the home. No matter how hungry, no one was to eat until all were seated and a prayer was prayed. There were times when it was not possible for all to eat together due to work and other pressing duties of the family. The following Swedish prayer was prayed by many families prior to meals when all were seated.

I Jesu namn till bords vi gå,
Välsigna Gud den mat vi få.
Gud till ära, oss till gagn,
Så få vi mat i Jesu Namn.
Amen

Traditions tells us the following prayer was prayed following each meal. No one left the table until the prayer was prayed.

För mat och dryck Dig vare tack, o Gud.
Lär oss att hålla Dina bud.
Amen

Other Swede families used this prayer prior to eating:

I Jesu namn gå vi till bord,
Äta, dricka på hans ord.
Gud till ära, oss till gagn,
Så få vi mat i Jesu namn.
Amen

By contrast in this modern age, families with busy schedules often manage to eat meals "on the "run." Some call it "grazing," helping yourself to food ready to eat on the table, stove, or in the refrigerator, whenever one has the time to eat.

We can only wonder what the immigrants would think of our meal habits today?

Chapter 19

MUSIC IN THE SMOKY VALLEY

When we read of music in the Smoky Valley in those very early years of the community, we note the Swedes brought with them to Kansas a deep heritage of great music. The Swedes, early on, established a culture of devotion to sacred music, which was soon to result in the now famous Messiah Chorus.

Dr. Bergin, in his first book, *Pioneer Swedish-American Culture,* writes: "Dr. Olof Olsson organized a choir in the fall of 1869 which sang publicly for the first time at the morning service New Years Day, 1870. The choir practiced faithfully in Dr. Olsson's home."

The following were members of this first choir: Mr. and Mrs. P. Fallquist, Mr. and Mrs. Carl Erickson, Mr. and Mrs. Carl Lindberg, Magnus Carlson, Mrs. Lincoln, Mr. and Mrs. Sven Bjorn, Mrs. O. Erickson, Israel Anderson, Mrs. Berg, Dr. Rundstrom, John A. Swenson, John E. Johnson, Emma Sandell, Elizabeth Anderson, and John E. Johnson." Dr. Bergin further states "E. Agrelius organized a band in 1877 with an orchestra starting the next year."

Dr. Lindquist states in his book, Smoky Valley People, "the auspicious beginning of Handel's Messiah had its beginning in 1882." Since the first rendition of the Messiah Chorus, the tradition has continued each year during Holy Week performing on Palm Sunday and again on Easter Sunday. The faithfulness of leaders and performers of the Messiah each year, gives evidence to the deep appreciation for sacred music of those who were members in the early days." However, the history and story of the Messiah in Lindsborg, will be left up to those who have more of an intimate knowledge of its history.

We note families grew rapidly during those early days in the Valley. Children were introduced to music early, with older members tutoring the young singing the Swedish hymns of the old country. Most children learned the English language only upon enrolling in the public schools where singing in the language of the new land, English, was encouraged. Music, particularly sacred music, was as important part of the fabric of the lives of these hardy Swede families.

Chapter 20

ADDITIONAL HISTORY TO BE PRESERVED

RAILROADS

The Kansas Pacific Railroad was the first, along with a depot in Lindsborg in 1880. Later this became the Union Pacific Railroad.

The Missouri Pacific Railroad and depot was built in 1887. This became the mainline from Kansas City to Pueblo, Colorado.

BRICK STREETS ON MAIN STREET

The first brick streets in Lindsborg were laid in 1917–1918. Interesting to note: A a strong vote of the City Council in 1967 was to overlay the brick streets with asphalt. This was defeated by a number of merchants led by Hilding Jaderborg, owner of Swedish Crafts on Main Street.

ELECTRICITY AND WATER

The first Electrical and Water plant brought light and water to the community in 1905.

FLOUR MILLS

The first Dam and Flour and Grist Mill was built in 1872 on the north bank of the Smoky Hill River. It was rebuilt in 1898 and named the Smoky Valley Roller Mill.

EARLY MANUFACTURING PLANT

The Hagstrom Manufacturing Company, built in 1907, was the first manufacturing company in the community employing around 105 people.

Chapter 21

TRADITIONS CONTINUED IN THE VALLEY

The Swedish immigrants who settled in the Smoky Valley brought with them traditions, habits and overall culture from the old country. We have pointed out, and again emphasize, family meals together around kitchen tables were almost sacred. These were evidently very happy and intimate family times with members sharing happenings and plans for the day and future.

Christmas was a special time of the year for these Swedes from the province of Värmland who were now adjusting to living so far from home in this new country.

Following days of planning and food preparation, the Christmas Eve noon meal, known as dopp i grytan (dip in the pot) officially commenced the days of celebrating the birth of the Saviour Jesus Christ.

On a following page is a description how the custom of dopp i grytan was carried out in those early days and is still celebrated each year in many homes where Swedish descendents live. *Cf Appendix, p. 99.*

The Christmas Evening meal continued the celebration with many Swedish delicacies, including lutfisk and ostkaka, along with many other Swedish recipe foods. Following the meal, as soon as dishes were cleared and washed, the family gathered around the Christmas tree to sing carols. Then to pacify the young family members it was time for the father of the house to read the Christmas story from Luke 2 followed by a brief prayer time. Only then was it time to open gifts.

Most of the family retired early, as on Christmas morning all would arise and make the trip by foot, or horse and wagon, to the church in all kinds of unpredictable Kansas weather in time for the 5:00 a.m. Julotta worship service.

Following a rather lengthy service, families would greet each other and head for their homes for a bountiful Swedish breakfast. Often in those early years families would also join at church for a late afternoon light Christmas supper and a time of singing and fellowship.

Chapter 22

CORONADO HEIGHTS

Coronado Heights, located three miles northwest of Lindsborg, could relate reams of stories about those early settlers, if it could only talk. Pleasant, exciting, shocking, interesting stories about the past one hundred and forty plus years will perhaps best be left untold by Coronado Heights.

Coronado Heights certainly must have drawn the early immigrants to its very top to view the many miles of tall grass and rolling hills. What a sight for them to write home about in those early days on the prairie. The Smoky Valley viewed from the top of this highest hill provided a gorgeous sight in the 1860s and certainly the same is true today.

Historians differ in identifying the route of Francisco Vasquez de Coronado, the famous Spanish explorer. It has been said, it is quite likely that the Smoky Valley was visited by the Spaniards in July 1541, so the recorded history of Lindsborg and Coronado Heights may have begun then rather than with the arrival of the first colonists.

The land including this highest hill was initially secured by the local historical society, part by purchase, and part by long-time lease, and now serves as a public park maintained by the Smoky Valley Historical Association. In turn, the high hill was officially named Coronado Heights.

A footpath was built, early on, to the summit on the southeast slope. This path was named "Olsson Trail," to honor the memory of the first leader of the settlers. Later a rough and winding road was built from the bottom to the top, six tenths of a mile, and is known as the Swensson Road in honor of the memory of Dr. Carl Swensson.

Chapter 23

HOBO CAMPS IN LINDSBORG

As most people could tell, "Hobos" are those out of work, vagrants and gentlemen who obviously had no permanent home, and who would move from town to town dependent upon the weather and the generosity of local residents.

But there is much more to it than that. Further, we must mention this story on Hobos in Lindsborg seems to fit between the first section of "Lindsborg Then" and the second section on "Lindsborg Now."

Those who have read a similar story on Hobos written by this writer in the local newspaper this past fall as part of the celebration of Lindsborg's 140th anniversary, have brought out two sides of the Hobo story which took place years ago in Lindsborg. There are a number of senior citizens we have interviewed, who remembered the days when Lindsborg was a haven for Hobos each summer, and had many stories to relate to experiences with these annual visitors to our city. And there are those younger folks who have expressed that they had never heard of Hobos in Lindsborg, and seemed delighted to hear about these unusual people.

Taken from an Encyclopedia, "Hobo is a term that refers to a subculture of wandering homeless people, particularly those who make a habit of hopping freight trains. The iconic image of Hobo is that of a downtrodden, shabbily dressed, and perhaps as a drunken male."

Hobos are depicted carrying a sack of some kind, and often seen asking for money, food, or work. The Hobo imagery has been employed by Entertainers to create characters in the past, two of them being Emmett Kelly's "Wierie Willie," and Red Skelton's "Freddy the Freeloader."

To depart from the Encyclopedia descriptions that depict Hobos, we add the following. Hobos were considered homeless tramps and vagrants who were not interested in holding steady jobs, or possibly were incapable of steady employment of any kind. Further, a Hobo could be one who simply decided that the Hobo life style was the way to live and see the country. Free transportation via rides on rail box cars took them wherever they decided to go, as by word of mouth they knew Hobo camps were available in most parts of the country. This was particularly true in small towns where they found courteous and generous people who would share their food.

In the early thirties and forties, and possibly earlier, Lindsborg seemed an attractive place for Hobos who usually found places along the Smoky Hill River bank to settle for a time during the warmer months. Two railroads came through Lindsborg, the Missouri Pacific and the Union Pacific. Hobos would often be seen riding on top of these box cars as the trains slowly made their way through the town. At times Hobos could be seen jumping off a train car, and at other times, when fall weather approached, Hobos were seen boarding a box car hoping to find a warmer climate.

During the warm months a number of Hobos would congregate on the south side of the Smoky Hill River, on the edge of Lindsborg, between the vehicle bridge and the railroad bridge which were a quarter mile apart. The Hobos through the years had cleared this area to set up their camp, where they would pitch small tents, and often had fires to warm their food if any was available. According to some

Hobos, a gentlemen's agreement was set up for all to share their possessions, the most important which was food. As many as five or six at a time could be seen cooking their meals, wading or swimming in the river, or lounging in their camp site.

Of course the Hobos would come and go during the spring, summer and fall, using rail cars as transportation to and from Lindsborg. Teenagers in Lindsborg at times took advantage of playing "Hobo" by hopping a slow moving box car for a ride through town.

We have been told, Hobos during this time in history, could be found throughout the country usually in small towns with rivers and railroads. Information by word of mouth obviously was shared that Lindsborg was a good place to spend some time with a good Hobo camp to welcome them. Lindsborg recognized that the Hobos usually arrived in May or June, and then completely vacated the camp by October.

Often Hobos were seen knocking on back doors of homes in Lindsborg, asking for food or possibly for work. According to Willis Olson, who grew up in Lindsborg and now resides here with his wife Marian, related that his father, Rev. Nels Olson, who served as Pastor of Messiah Lutheran Church in Lindsborg during the thirties and forties.

Willis goes on to state: "Pastor Olson and Dr. Alfred Bergin, long-time Pastor of Bethany Lutheran Church in Lindsborg, compiled lists of homes that were willing to provide food when Hobos came to their back doors. Lists of these homes found their way to the Hobo camp in south Lindsborg." Is it any wonder Lindsborg became such a popular place for these transient gentlemen?

Coincidentally, teenagers found what they termed the best place for swimming in the river very near the Hobo camp. In fact, for years a diving board was located on the north bank of the river. The writer of this story was one of those teenagers who spent time in this area. The Hobos seemed to enjoy our company and we learned both bad and good from them.

Never did we hear of any trouble or damage caused by the Hobos. They were, by and large, friendly and enjoyed the young swimmers who used the Smoky as their swimming pool. For years this was a popular place to swim until Lindsborg built its first pool in 1948.

It is with some regret, for some of us living in Lindsborg during these times, that we did not make more of an effort to become personally acquainted with so many interesting gentlemen. Some we are sure would have fabulous stories to tell about their lives.

Where have all the Hobos gone?

We fear they are the homeless now who prefer living in the large cities of our country.

CONCLUSION OF LINDSBORG THEN

Dr. Emory Lindquist, a former President of Bethany College, in his book *Smoky Valley People*, states "nothing pointed with certainty a large settlement, in mid-Kansas, until a young 28-year-old Lutheran Pastor, the Rev. Olof Olsson, made the decision that he and friends would immigrate to America and Kansas in the middle of a strange country arriving in the summer of 1869."

Alf Brorson of Torsby, Sweden, in his book published in Swedish, *Vägen Till Lindsborg* (The Road to Lindsborg), states "these Swedish emigrants coming to America and to the Lindsborg area were not the very poor indigents, but had some financial means to assist in settling the Smoky Valley. The poor in Sweden could not afford the trip over, and the rich were too well-off financially to consider such a move."

Today when we travel, especially the country roads of the Smoky Valley, we find it almost unreal and mind-boggling as we witness the gorgeous fields of grain, the well-kept farmsteads, and feel and enjoy the clean pure air of this area in the middle of our great country.

So many stories are gone forever on the settling of this community due to the dearth of recorded history. Will we ever really know why the community of Lindsborg was settled right here in the middle of the Smoky Valley? Still, we can be thankful for the books by early writers who bring us many facts we can compile in order to preserve the history of this place.

As we conclude the *Lindsborg Then* part of this book, we must mention, that for quite some time we have wondered why someone has not made a movie of the settling of

Lindsborg, here in the Smoky Valley of Kansas, and possibly tracing its over 140 years of existence.

For now, it is on to the second half of these writings (*Lindsborg Now*).

LINDSBORG
NOW

Year 2010

Chapter 24

LINDSBORG NOW IN 2010

Lindsborg today is still commonly thought of as a center of Swedish-American life and culture, with a number of residents still having strong ties to those first hardy immigrants who settled this community. Over the years it has had a steady, but slow growth in population with the City Hall reporting there are now 3,417 in the population of Lindsborg.

Never has the community been more enthusiastic than today, about the value of preserving the Swedish heritage and traditions of the Smoky Valley that dates back over 140 years ago.

Gone are the days of only common Swedish names such as Peterson, Larson, Olson, Nelson, Carlson, Lindquist, Lindholm, and Johnson. Those names are still common, but the phone book also lists names like Achenbach, Allsbury, Bellah, Crawford, DeWitt, Kelly, and Jones.

Of further interest we note, it was a non-Swede, Dr. William Holwerda, who instigated the celebration of the first Hyllningsfest in 1941 to pay tribute to pioneers who made Lindsborg happen.

The celebration is held every other year in the month of October. During this celebration of the Swedish heritage, many local residents wear Swedish costumes, tents are filled with vendors selling their wares, and an abundance of Swedish food is available along with an authentic Smörgåsbord. Anywhere one goes during this time they are sure to hear Swedish music being played and sung, and also may enjoy a large number of art studios. A two-mile long parade is part of the Saturday morning enjoyment, with the Bethany College Homecoming football game to follow in the afternoon. As an important opening of the festival is a Thursday evening worship service which those early settlers would certainly appreciate.

A number of other celebrations are held each year in the community, including Midsummers Day in June, St. Lucia in December, a gala July 4th musical talent performance in Swensson Park, and a May celebration in the Old Mill Park.

On a tour of the city one will note Dala Horses on the front of homes which also adds to the Swedish heritage and tradition of the community. Most of these horses have been made by Hemslöjd here in Lindsborg. Owner of this business, Ken Swisher, reports, as of June 2010, just over 35,000 dala horses have been produced by the business. The Hemslöjd, along with a number of local establishments, specialize in the sale of Scandinavian items. Consequently, the Dala Horse has become the "name plate" of the community of Lindsborg.

We must confess some of the writings in this part, *Lindsborg Now*, will be at times somewhat repetitious, as we attempt to present a picture of Lindsborg the way it is today. Much of what we have here now had its origin in the early years of Lindsborg.

Chapter 25

EDUCATION IN LINDSBORG ALWAYS HIGH PRIORITY

The Swedish immigrants brought with them from Sweden a high priority for education. Since its first school in 1870, held in a building in the center of town called the "Ark," the public school system has flourished.

Today, 140 plus years later, Lindsborg has a fine public school system with excellent facilities, numbering 1,004 students in the fall of 2009, K through the 12th grade with 70 more in a charter school. Each student from fifth grade through the senior year is issued a computer for their use. Lindsborg High School is classified as a 4-A School.

In 1986, with school consolidation, the Falun, Smolan, Roxbury and Marquette communities joined the school district named Smoky Valley (USD 400).

Bethany College commenced serving post high school students and adults in 1881, using Bethany Lutheran Church for classes. The Swedish immigrants did not come to the Smoky Valley as itinerants but as settlers to share in the life fully in the new community. Higher education was rated high with these settlers who sought a better life for their children.

Bethany College, a Lutheran school, which has been cherished among the American public through the years, has witnessed the forces of change throughout its history. Today the rich heritage of Bethany is noted by the renditions of the Messiah and Bach during Holy Week each year, when people come from far and wide to enjoy the music of a college and community, some of whom travel distances for weekly rehearsals.

In this school year there are around 600 students enrolled in Bethany College, which has enjoyed a magnificent change on campus in buildings and grounds during the past two years.

Chapter 26

CELEBRATIONS

In Lindsborg in this present era, a celebration is presently being held, or a celebration has just finished, or one is being planned. Swedes who visit from the old country tell us all Swedes love to celebrate in Sweden so maybe Lindsborg is just following the pattern.

The every other year Hyllningsfest is celebrated in October, and is the most well-known of the many festivals held in Lindsborg. It began in 1941, when local physician Dr. William Holwerda instigated the celebration of the heritage of the community. The festival includes a parade, a football game at Bethany College, food booths, craft tents with a variety of items for sale, reunions, and oh yes, a popular Smörgåsbord, and an abundance of Swedish style music. Often Swedish groups from out of state, and occasionally from Sweden, are in attendance to entertain and be entertained.

Millfest is held in early May at the Old Mill near the Smoky Hill River. This is the one time of the year the flour mill is in operation for visitors to view.

The Old Mill museum is an added attraction open all year. Food again is plentiful, along with usually quaint and different music.

Midsummers Day weekend, with seemingly more activities each year, is celebrated in June with music in the park, along with craft booths and choices of food. A Maypole dance in the park is held in the evening, followed by a street dance on Main Street.

July 4 is celebrated by most communities, but we dare say, few do it like Lindsborg, with an old-fashioned program of quality music in the park, along with food to enjoy, followed by an entertaining fireworks display on most years.

The month of December brings the annual St. Lucia festival of music, with the crowning of a young teenage queen selected by the high school Swedish Dancers.

Chapter 27

SMOKY VALLEY HISTORICAL ASSOCIATION

The S.V.H.A. has its roots dating back to the 1920s when the earliest improvements to Coronado Heights took place. The Association is a registered non-profit organization, and is free and clear title holder to the land on which Coronado is located. Even though Coronado is located just into Saline County, the Association is based in McPherson County in Lindsborg.

The S.V.H.A. is responsible for the maintenance and operation of Coronado Heights with a few simple rules for its use. Further, the Association has accepted the responsibility for the installation of twenty-three permanent historical signs on the Välkommen Trail, built in 2006 over an abandoned rail through the city, which has enhanced the preservation of local history.

The Association continues to participate in a number of celebrations in Lindsborg each year. Monthly meetings are held (with the exception of the summer months) to which any and all are welcome to attend. Membership contributions are the main source of funding. A free will donation in any amount will secure membership in the Association for the year. Membership is renewed in the first quarter of each year.

Significant donations are received from time to time with a specific project in mind.

The Smoky Valley Historical Association's mission statement states, that "the purpose of this Association shall be to collect, arrange and preserve historical data, books, pamphlets and manuscripts pertaining to the early history and settlement of our community in general, and the City of Lindsborg in particular; to preserve and beautify places of historical interest in our community and its vicinity; and to promote the study of history of our settlement and its culture by lectures and other available means."

Chapter 28

CORONADO HEIGHTS TODAY

Today, Coronado Heights, located three miles northwest of Lindsborg, still stands as magically as ever, overlooking the town of Lindsborg and the Smoky Valley. The scenery from the top of this hill is ever-changing with the seasons of the year. The greening of the fields in March and April and the sight of combines reaping the harvest in the fields in June and July are simply magnificent to view.

The maintenance of Coronado Heights is the responsibility of the Smoky Valley Historical Association with special mention of Dr. Duane Fredrickson, a long-time Lindsborg Physician, who has made it his project to almost weekly check and clean up the picnic areas and the fort on the top of the hill for many years.

WPA work project during the mid 1930s made possible the building of a number of picnic areas constructed of native rock and cement including places to cook and barbecue. Further, it was at this time a castle was built of sandstone on the top, as well as bathrooms. Work today is ongoing to rebuild some of these areas, along with needed improvement of the winding road from bottom to top, which is six tenths of a mile.

Two primitive-appearing trails have been laid out from top to bottom of both the east and the southwest sides of Coronado. These trails are used for hiking and at times for bicycles. Competitive races are held from time to time on these trails for bicycles with entries from far and wide.

Coronado Heights has proven through the years as a popular picnic area with permanent tables and benches of cement and rock from which to enjoy the views while feasting on the food of choice. Traffic on the road up the hill gets almost daily use, except for in extremely inclement weather, by sightseers and for those planning a picnic or party.

As Chris Abercrombie of Lindsborg has pointed out, "today Coronado Heights has hundreds of visitors each month, making it one of the most popular destinations in Central Kansas. People from all over Kansas, and other states and foreign countries can be found exploring the hill on any given day."

Coronado Heights perhaps brings more vivid memories of picnic times on the hill for senior citizens who grew up in the days when Coronado was the place to go for a family picnic. Coronado picnics have pretty well been replaced by backyard barbecues in the more recent times. However, most who have enjoyed Coronado Heights would agree with the recent selection of Coronado Heights as one of the 8 Wonders of Kansas in the category of Geography.

Chapter 29

LINDSBORG CITY ORGANIZATIONS

THE LOCAL CHAMBER OF COMMERCE has provided services in the community for more than 80 years, and remains central to the economic and cultural spirit of Lindsborg and the Smoky Valley. The Chamber has recently taken on a new program to enhance the business community, and coordinates activities with the local Convention and Visitors Bureau.

THE LINDSBORG CONVENTION AND VISITORS BUREAU has as its goal "to ensure that visitors to Lindsborg have the most enjoyable experience possible. They are a clearing house for information on events, organizations, and local businesses. Visitors get help with their lodging needs, dining options, and entertainment chores. Staffed with local residents, the CVB also provides insight into the history and Swedish culture of Lindsborg."

THE SMOKY VALLEY COMMUNITY FOUNDATION, founded in 2002 has greatly increased financial assistance for non-profit organizations throughout the Smoky Valley which covers southern Saline and northern McPherson County, including Lindsborg, Marquette, Bridgeport, Roxbury, Smolan, Falun and Assaria.

The mission of the Foundation is "to establish endowments that enhance the quality of life for current and future generations by reinvesting in the Smoky Valley." The Foundation is governed by a volunteer board and is among ten community foundations affiliated with the Greater Salina Community Foundation for endowment fund investments and management.

Smoky Valley non-profit organizations are welcome to apply for grants which are awarded in the spring and fall of the year. Further, individuals are encouraged to consider being involved in giving to the organization to be invested in endowments of their choice.

SISTER CITIES LINDSBORG AND MUNKFORS, SWEDEN have cooperated since 1991 which has added to tourist travel for both cities, and also to develop a closer relationship between the two countries. The Sister City committee consists of seven members appointed by the Mayor, with the consent of the City Council. Our sister city is Munkfors in the province of Värmland, Sweden: "The committee is responsible for strengthening social, cultural and economic ties with our sister city."

THE BRIDGE MAGAZINE, now THE SWEDEN & AMERICA MAGAZINE, has included numerous articles on Lindsborg and the Smoky Valley during the past twenty years. Mr. Alf Brorson of Torsby, Sweden has been the major author of these informative articles. A few of the past articles have also been written by present local residents.

Further, Mr. Brorson continues to have articles published in the local News-Record and has adopted Lindsborg as his second home. A few years ago he was honored when he received an honorary Citizen of Lindsborg award. He made his 17th visit to this area in the summer of 2010.

THE LIONS, KIWANIS, and ROTARY clubs are today all active in our community. These service clubs support the town in a number of ways, as well as providing fellowship and educational programs for members.

The Lions Club, organized in 1924, meets biweekly; the Rotary, organized in 1936, and Kiwanis Club, organized in 1948, meet weekly.

BROADWAY R.F.D. has proven for many years to be a very popular summer theatre. In fact it is the longest running summer theatre in Kansas, performing a variety of musicals in July each year since 1959. The July performances in Swensson Park has been the place to be on a summer evening, with plenty of food, including home made ice-cream and soft drinks for all to enjoy.

THE AMERICAN-SCANDINAVIAN ASSOCIATION has for a long time been an active participant in the community to preserve the heritage of the entire Smoky Valley. Mr. A. John Pearson, having served again as President of the organization, has been a tireless worker in keeping the club active, and Dr. Duane Fredrickson, recently retired local Physician, was elected as the new President of the organization. Special events are held several times each year.

A minimal membership fee is required which brings a quarterly publication in the mail.

THE LINDSBORG SWEDISH CLUB meets weekly on Friday mornings at 10:00 in the Bethany Lutheran Church with Julie Neywick serving as a faithful President. The group was started around fifteen years ago with Mrs. Inga-Lill Eliason and Rev. Martin Ringstrom the organizers. Mrs. Eliason, who was born in Sweden, continues as a regular member in her early nineties. Rev. Ringstrom continued to attend weekly past his 100th birthday.

Weekly meetings consist of a variety of programs including Swedish lessons, speakers, occasional pot luck dinners, and with an open welcome to all interested in preserving the Swedish heritage in the Smoky Valley.

THE LINDSBORG SWEDISH DANCERS have long been a popular part of the heritage of the community and the

Smoky Valley. The adult dance group entertains at Hyllningsfests, Midsummers Day celebrations, and when called on to perform in the community. In addition, the group has made many trips to Colorado and other states, as well as to many Kansas communities to perform....

The High School Dancers are equally well received throughout the community during the many celebrations. This group has made a number of trips to Sweden to perform in several localities. The Dancers' schedule calls for a tour of Sweden every fourth year.

THE DALA HORSE is frequently used as a symbol in Swedish settlements of the USA. Horses were originally carved from wood in the Dalarna province of Sweden, and are now highly popular, particularly with those of Swedish descent in our country.

Colorful Dala Horses can be seen hanging from houses and doorfronts in Lindsborg, and also from the fronts of businesses, and they can be found even on the sides of local police vehicles. The Horse was designed by Ken Sjogren and then marketed with his partner Ken Swisher in the Hemslöjd, located in the business district of Lindsborg.

It has been designated as the official seal of the community.

Chapter 30

CHURCHES IN LINDSBORG

Lindsborg today has seven churches in which to worship.

Bethany Lutheran Church was the first to organize in 1869, shortly after the first immigrants settled here. Building of the first church commenced shortly after the settlers arrived here in the Smoky Valley, giving evidence of strong Christian beliefs.

The Evangelical Mission Covenant Church began holding services in homes in the early 1870s and was officially organized in the late 1800s.

Messiah Lutheran Church was organized in 1908.

The Swedish Methodist Church was organized in a school house in November, 1871 with nine charter members with Rev. W. Peterson as Pastor.

The organization of the Lindsborg Baptist Church took place in the home of P. E. Anderson on November 3, 1880 under the leadership of Rev. August Anderson, a traveling missionary.

The St. Bridget Catholic Church has held regular Sunday morning worship in Lindsborg since 1981.

The Smoky Valley Independent Baptist Church was established in 1999.

TACOL

The Associated Churches in Lindsborg (TACOL) work nicely together, sponsoring the following projects.

RELEASED BIBLE SCHOOL TIME, in operation since the mid-1920s has been an important undertaking in spreading the Gospel in the community. Initially children would report to the church of their choice on Wednesday mornings for learning more about the Bible. However, in past years all third and fourth grade students have classes in the Covenant Church and all fifth and sixth graders in Bethany Lutheran Church. Each church in the community is responsible for supplying teachers. The two churches mentioned are within a block of the public school. Released School Time is optional for all children, with presently about two thirds of the children participating.

A THRIFT STORE, operated by TACOL, located in a former bowling alley in the northeast part of town is a busy place for shoppers and people bringing clothing and other items for the store to sell at low prices. This place of business has had a major growth in the past years with the majority of workers volunteers.

SPECIAL CITY WIDE WORSHIP SERVICES sponsored by TACOL are as follows: Annual Mayor's Prayer Breakfast held in early Spring; Hyllningsfest Thursday night worship to commence the festival; Annual Good Friday service; A thanksgiving service held on the eve of Thanksgiving Day; World Day of Prayer.

Financial assistance for the poor, indigent is always available from TACOL. The organization does accept donations for this purpose.

BETHANY HOME

Bethany Home is an all-encompassing living facility, complete with duplexes, apartments, and in-house living. Licensed by the state as An Intermediate Care Facility, residents of the Home have the opportunity for many indoor and outdoor activities. Staff enjoy taking residents out to local entertainment and many performers will bring their shows to Bethany Home. A chapel is located within the facility and provides regular worship services for residents as well as community members. Artists often display their work throughout the hallways, making them living galleries.

The Home first opened its doors in November, 1911 for eleven elderly residents as an adult care facility. Bethany Home continues to be owned and operated by the Central States Synod of the Evangelical Lutheran Church of America (ELCA).

Chapter 31

RECREATIONAL FACILITIES

The city of Lindsborg provides city parks with up-dated recreational facilities, including a swimming pool, and bandshell for concerts and other performances in a delightful setting. The town is a strong tennis community with fourteen courts located in the city. Recently the Ron Dahlsten Tennis Complex at the high school was dedicated, which is becoming the envy of tennis enthusiasts far and wide. Further, the Smoky Hill River provides fishing for those who enjoy this activity.

The Välkommen walking and bicycling trail, which became a reality in 2006 of two and one half miles, splits the town being installed on a former railroad bed. Nearly two dozen signs along the trail relate the story of earliest times in the community. Booklets with stories of these signs are available on the trail and a number of businesses in town.

A nine-hole grass green golf course is located two miles from the city limits which is open for membership or green fees. This course was laid out in the mid 1950s under the leadership of Coach Ray D. Hahn, long-time coach of all sports at Bethany College.

Villa Ro Apartments, located on the east side of Lindsborg, operates as a low-cost Housing Authority of the Department of Housing and urban Development (HUD). The complex is made up of 35 duplex structures (70 apartments) which range in size from one to three bedrooms.

Four units are equipped for wheelchairs and include handicapped showers.

A Community Room building is available to tenants, and as an extension of their living room it also features a piano, TV, tables and chairs to accommodate 60, and a fully stocked kitchen.

Lindsborg has been referred to many times as "*A Shoppers' Delight*" with a number of unique stores selling Scandinavian items along with many of other wares. With the recent honors received by the city, designated as one of the 8 Wonders of Kansas by the Kansas Sampler Foundation in four categories, visitor and tourist travel is expected to increase. The four 8 Wonders categories cited earlier, are in the areas of History, Art, Geography and Commerce (traditional Kansas pop art customs).

Chapter 32

KING CARL GUSTAF'S VISIT TO LINDSBORG, APRIL 17, 1976

Visitors are always welcome and encouraged to visit Lindsborg, with its strong Swedish atmosphere, which has been an attraction for many to visit. Especially in the past thirty years tourist travel to the community has experienced a noticeable increase. Dating back to 1976, when the King of Sweden came for a visit, the town became a place to visit for tourists from Sweden as well as from our country.

In late 1975 it was announced locally, that a very special Swede was planning a visit to our community. The King of Sweden, King Carl XVI Gustaf would really be visiting on April 17, 1976. A score of hot and old rumors kept the town gossip at high pitch regarding this possibility.

Even though local authorities assured all that the King of Sweden's plans to visit America included an appearance in Lindsborg, there was much skepticism that this would actually take place. A good deal of coffee table conversation in early 1976 centered around the Swedish King's coming to little Lindsborg on the plains of Kansas. After all, how many small towns such as Lindsborg, ever had a King of country visit their community.

Serving as Administrator of Bethany Home in Lindsborg at this time, it was a thrill to know that the Home would be the first place for the King to visit, due to the fact nine present residents and two staff members were born in Sweden, and that the majority of the other residents were of Swedish descent and were able to speak the Swedish language with a varying degree of proficiency.

During the two-week period prior to the King's visit, a number of Swedish press, journalists and television personalities came to Bethany Home as part of the preparation. The great number of fluent-speaking Swedes living in the Home, of course, was a drawing card for the Swedish press. Two in particular acquired a close affinity for the folks in the Home in the persons of Miss Christine Liljcrantz and Mr. Hans Persson. One was a journalist and the other a photographer. The two visiting Swedes spent many hours interviewing, in particular, the native born Swedes living in the Home.

Albert Berquist, one of the Home's quaint and lovable residents living on the second floor of Pioneer Memorial, had been born in Sweden and immigrated to America and the Smoky Valley when he was eighteen years old. "Berky," as we all affectionately referred to him, had retained his delightful and quaint Swedish accent throughout the years of farming north of Lindsborg, where he and his wife and family of three sons, Warren, Carroll, and Arden lived. "Berky" was the first of the Home's residents interviewed by Miss Liljcrantz and Mr. Persson who asked if he was getting excited about the King of Sweden's impending visit. This fine old Swede with a good sense of humor, took his time in answering, then with grave concern showing, replied in his beautiful accent, "Hail No, vi do you tink I came to dis country? It vas to get avay from de damn King!"

Later during the interview the Swedish visitors pressed "Berky" for his age which he usually kept secret. At first he refused, then with more grave concern replied again, in his special accent, "Vell, I tink I vas born in eighteen eighty-tree, but I don't know if dat vas before Christ, or after Christ."

On April 17, following several hours of waiting, King Carl Gustaf appeared with his entourage into the packed Bethany Home, with the nine residents and two staff members who were born in Sweden waiting around a special table for his visit. And yes, one was Albert "Berky" Berquist, scrubbed and dressed in his very best, and with a twinkle in his eye he shook the King's hand. Giving the King an official greeting that day was Mr. C. A. Berggren, a ninety-two-year old native Swede whose message in Swedish was: "I have seen you before, twenty years ago, when my wife and I were visiting Sweden. We were brought to the King's court yard and several small boys were playing in the nude, and you were pointed out as the next King of Sweden."

A remark the twenty-four-year old King would be sure to remember for a very long time.

The King and his group left the Home that day for Presser Hall on the campus of Bethany College, where the famed Messiah Chorus was waiting to perform for him.

On this rainy day, the King was officially greeted at the South Park in the Old Mill Complex.

Chapter 33

VISIT OF THE MOTALA CHOIR

Following the April 17, 1976 visit of the King of Sweden, it seemed to be the custom of visitors from Sweden to visit Lindsborg, the little town they had heard about in their own country.

It was July 5, 1977 when A. John Pearson from Bethany College called on this very warm summer afternoon in Kansas to ask if Bethany Home would be interested in hosting a group of singers from Sweden for afternoon coffee in the Home. He explained the group of 44 Swedes, known as the Motala Chamber Choir from near Stockholm, had arrived in town and would be singing that evening in Bethany Lutheran Church. Of course we were delighted and happy to have these Swedes visit, as our residents loved to meet and chat with persons from the old country. Many of the Home's Swedes still had close family members living in Sweden. Even though it was quite early in the afternoon and many of our residents were napping, we announced over the intercom we were having a large group of guests from Sweden in a few minutes in our dining room. Our staff was urged to bring those who spoke Swedish well to the dining room where we would be serving coffee, tea and probably some delicacies.

The group arrived by charter bus with the choir consisting of forty-four singers of varying ages. We found out rather quickly that this group of Swedes, unlike most Scandinavians, spoke very little English. This of course presented some problems initially, until we managed to seat them in our dining room with one or two of our Swedish-speaking residents at each table.

Things went well until we noticed one table of Swedish singers and no Bethany Home residents. Wanting so much to make these people from the old country feel welcome, I hurried to their table and proceeded to select the kindliest looking Swede, placed my hand on his shoulder, and addressed the young man with my best Swedish, which is quite limited. "Jag kan forsta lite svenska, men jag kan inte tala mycket svenska." (I can understand a little Swedish, but I cannot talk much Swedish). This gentle-appearing young blond man looked up at me with the strangest stare and said, "Hey Buddy, don't talk that Swedish to me. I'm the bus driver."

Chapter 34

MAJOR HAPPENINGS "NOW" IN 2010

A major happening occurred in Lindsborg on April 2, 2010 when a sales tax increase was successful by 29 votes, 635 to 606, with 78 percent of eligible voters mailing in their ballots.

The 2010 sales tax initiative included ½ cent sales tax to pick up when the local hospital sales tax expires in the spring, which is to retire the hospital debt on its building.

Secondly, a portion of the next ½ cent tax will be used to renovate the Sundstrom Building's first floor into a community conference center as well as funds for infrastructure in improving streets and other projects. The Sundstrom building erected in 1898 is by far the largest building in downtown Lindsborg.

Further, this vote included a reduction of property taxes by 3 mills. The vote for the sales tax increase will:

1. Stabilize future property taxes.
2. Help retire the hospital debt.
3. Enable capital improvements,
4. Help to avoid major cuts in city services.

The vote was close and contentious, with only the future being able to judge how successful or unsuccessful.

During the past few years Lindsborg has been honored by a statewide study and selection process in four of six areas: Kansas Art, Kansas Commerce, Kansas Customs, and Kansas Geography.

In October of 2008 the Birger Sandzén Gallery was honored as one of the 8 Wonders of Kansas Art.

In March of 2009 the Hemslöjd was honored as one of the 8 Wonders of Kansas Commerce.

In October 2009 the Dala Horses of Kansas were honored as one of the 8 Wonders of Customs (traditional and pop art).

In February 2010 Coronado Heights was honored as one of the 8 Wonders of Geography.

In addition, Dr. Duane Fredrickson, long-time Lindsborg Physician, was honored in March 2009 by being named Kansas Family Physician of the year by the Academy of Kansas Physicians.

LINDSBORG VÄLKOMMEN TRAIL

In June of this year the Smoky Valley Historical Association completed signage of historical markers along the two-and-one-half mile walking and bicycling trail, laid over rail beds which intersect the city of Lindsborg. Installation of these signs brought to 23 the number of markers, adding to the rich narrative of the community's strong heritage.

In addition, the Historical Association has published an up-dated edition of the illustrated booklet that documents the Association's Välkommen Trail signage project. The free 26-page booklet offers photographs and small narratives, and the community history that the project celebrates. The original booklet, published in 2007, listed 17 signs.

The most recent signs installed along the trail are as follows:

History of the Lindsborg Public Schools
Red Barn Studio

Lindsborg Evangelical Covenant Church
Art in Lindsborg
Hobo Camps on the Smoky
Messiah Lutheran Church

Signs installed previously are as follows:

Brief History of Early Lindsborg
Terrible Swedes football history
Bethany College
Birger Sandzén Gallery
Messiah Chorus
Bethany Lutheran Church
Railways to Highways
Mid KS Coop
The Power Plant
Missouri Pacific Railroad and Depot
Site of Many Uses
Home Studio of Anton Pearson
Hagstrom Manufacturing Company
Crossing the Smoky – Old Railroad Bridge
The Swedish Pavilion
Smoky Valley Ro1ler Mill
Crescent Flour Mill
Kansas Pacific Railroad and Depot

The Historical Association's new and up-dated booklet carries the original title, *Välkommen Trail – Exploring History Along Lindsborg's Välkommen Trail*, with a blue cover (the original was Swedish lemon yellow). The publication, with text and historical photographs, is free and may be obtained at numerous Lindsborg locations, including the News-Record. Each of the 2 x 3 feet historical markers is sponsored by a local business or by individual donors.

Corky Malm, Chairman of the Trail Sign Committee, has stated, "without the railroads Lindsborg would not be here today. The 1860s and 1870s in the Smoky Valley were quite difficult: people lived in dugouts, caves or hurriedly erected wooden shelters. Food, such as flour, sugar, and supplies, had to be purchased in Salina, and carried to Lindsborg on people's or animals' backs, or by sharing a neighbor's lumber wagon and team of horses or oxen. The trip could take three days."

Malm went on to state, "railroads were being built later across Kansas, and in 1878 a branch of the Union Pacific from Salina to McPherson was built. This was the most vital part of making the town prosper. Materials could come by rail. Houses, businesses and factories sprang forth. The town grew and thrived."

CONCLUSION

This concludes our work on *Lindsborg Then & Lindsborg Now*. By compiling information from books and writings of Dr. Alfred Bergin, Dr. Emory Lindquist and the written works of Alf Brorson of Torsby, Sweden and A. John Pearson of Lindsborg, we have attempted to bring together the stories of the early settling of the community of Lindsborg, Kansas. Hopefully the insights, facts and experiences of those early Smoky Valley immigrants will serve as preservation of the history of not only Lindsborg, but also of the Smoky Valley.

Much of the information pertinent to this study is the result of the research and writings in books and articles of the first writers of the settling of this area of our state. The two earliest writers, Dr. Alfred Bergin in the early 1900s and Dr. Emory Lindquist in the 1940s and 1950s, left us with facts and credence to the results of this writing. Mr. Alf Brorson followed in the late 1990s and early 2000s with his contribution of research and history included in his articles about the Smoky Valley during his many visits to Lindsborg, which numbered seventeen with this summer 2010 visit to our community. Brorson, an honorary citizen of Lindsborg, first visited Lindsborg in 1993.

Other sources, as you may note in the Source page, have proven valuable also in this compilation. Attempts have been made to document well the happenings, dates, places and people who had important parts in selecting the site on which Lindsborg is now located, along with telling the story of how immigrants from Sweden settled in this community.

Had it not been for the writings of these gentlemen, much of Lindsborg's earliest history would be lost forever. We take note here, Dr. Lindquist stated "the Swedish immigrants were people who established themselves economically and established themselves well; they became great and fine citizens." This fact can be well documented for it is unlikely the community of Lindsborg and the Smoky Valley would be what it is today. Without doubt there are hundreds of "nuggets" of local history which need to be written before they are allowed to die, as many facts of this area are already forgotten. We can note here that even early writers made minimal errors in citing years, people and places.

The second part of this book deals with Lindsborg Now, and has been compiled from numerous conversations, and facts supplied by the city, organizations, clubs and people. During my over twenty years as the Administrator of Bethany Home here in Lindsborg, the kindly precious souls who called the Home their home for a time, proved a "gold mine" of information gleaned regarding early days of the community. They enjoyed nothing more than to "Talk about the Old Days" of the past. Granted, much more information could be included in telling the *Lindsborg Then & Lindsborg Now* story, however we will leave those writings to those who might be so inclined to follow.

We have been told many times by Swedes visiting from Sweden and by those who live in our America that "Lindsborg undoubtedly is better known in Sweden than in our country."

As a closure, good friend "Corky" Malm relates his story of his and his wife's attendance at a large construction conference in Hawaii several years ago. At breakfast one morning guests were introducing themselves by name and where they were from. There were towns like Miami, Florida, Chicago, Illinois, and Denver, Colorado. "Corky" explained he was from a very small town in Kansas. A persistent lady asked: "Just where in Kansas?" "Corky" explained further by saying his little town was between Wichita and Salina,

Kansas. The lady then replied; "I know where Wichita is, but have never heard of Salina, but is it anywhere near Lindsborg?"

History not recorded, is perhaps history lost.

SOURCES FOR THIS PRESENTATION

Pioneer Swedish American Culture in Central Kansas; Dr. Alfred Bergin
The Smoky Valley in the After Years; Dr. Alfred Bergin
Smoky Valley People; Dr. Emory Lindquist
Vägen till Lindsborg; Alf Brorson
Swedes in America; Percy Hildebrand
Return to Ellis Island; Martin Antioun
The Bridge magazine articles; Alf Brorson
Other writings of Dr. Alfred Bergin
Bethany Lutheran Church historical records
Bethany Lutheran Church membership records
Conversations with A. John Pearson, Smoky Valley historian
Conversations with Paul Carlson years ago regarding family records
Conversations with, and genealogy records of John Hallqvist of Sweden
Conversations with Alf Brorson, teacher, historian, writer of Sweden
The Swedish American Center (formerly The Emigration Institute) of Karlstad, Sweden
Ken Sjogren family history settling in the Smoky Valley
Larry Elmquist, great-grandson of early Smoky Valley immigrant
Charlotte Ternstrom for church records
History of Marquette; Alan Lindfors and Eleanor Burnison
Carla Wilson, City of Lindsborg Convention and Vistors Bureau
Conversations with city officials
The Lindsborg News-Record

APPENDIX

4

DOPPA I GRYTAN PARTY? WHAT IS THAT?

BILL AND DORIS CARLSON EXPLAIN IT ALL

This Christmas Eve Day custom has been in the Carlson family for many years. Magnus and Maria Carlson and A. W. and Mathilda Carlson brought this custom with them from Varmland, Sweden in 1868. The Magnus Carlson homestead was one mile north and one mile west of Lindsborg and the A. W. Carlson farm a mile south of Coronado Heights.

Translated Doppa I Grytan means 'dipping in the pot' and this is exactly what is done during the Christmas Eve Day noon meal.

In Sweden a kettle of broth was kept on the back of the stove throughout Christmas Eve Day. Family members would help themselves to long slices of home made rye bread and dip into the hot broth whenever they became hungry or when they had time. This relieved the busy Mother of the household as she continued with preparations for the evening meal and other meals to be served on Christmas Day.

Since those early days here in Lindsborg in our family the Christmas Eve Doppa I Grytan has become a production and a most looked forward to Christmas event. Close friends are often invited to share in this festive occasion and to burn their tongues right along with our family members.

We always attempt to follow some rules of the meal, which we must confess, are often broken. No one is to sit down during the meal. Following the sounding of a very loud bell, and a Swedish table prayer, we are to line up buffet style loading our plates with beef and pork, along with salad, herring and extra long slices of homemade rye bread with butter.

The next step is to move past the stove with the piping hot, mouth watering broth, stopping to dip our bread and then move on quickly. From there it is an informal; but on your feet, mingling, chatting, dipping and yes, unintentional burning of tongues which is sure to happen on the first, second, or third bites.

Only the faint of heart and those not fully into the custom are soon out of the parade to the kettle on the stove. Others continue the parade as they remember it will be another year before we once again enjoy this quaint Swedish custom.

While growing up mince meat pie, and apple pie heaped with good country whipped cream awaited those who had used some common sense. Only now do the official rules allow the participants to sit down while attempting to enjoy their pie. In recent years the pie has been replaced with rice pudding, a delightful tray of holiday season cookies and candy. Always there has been plenty of good Swedish Egg Coffee available.

Finally in the midst of the Doppa I Grytan meal, we always remember our parents and other family members who are no longer with us who loved this custom so much. And also we as a family recognize that other segments of our family are enjoying this custom at exactly the same time in Lincoln, Nebraska; Kansas City, Kansas; Topeka, Kansas and on occasion in Tampa, Florida.

And, yes, there are drawbacks to this much looked forward to tradition of Doppa I Grytan. The evening meal that day doesn't seem quite as appealing. And with a scorched tongue can you blame us?????

Alf Brorson, Torsby Sweden 'dipping'

Recipe for

Doppa I Grytan

4 pounds lean beef

2 pounds lean pork

Salt meat three to four days before using. Cover with water and keep refrigerated.

The day of serving, wash off salt, cover with water, and add salt to taste. Add pepper and bay leaf and boil slowly all morning.

Remove meat and slice.

The kettle of broth is now ready for dipping.

The Lindsborg News-Record 2005 Special Christmas Section.

Doris (née Soderstrom) and Bill Carlson, Lindsborg, Kansas.

Smoky Valley skyscape.

Smoky Hill River.

CPSIA information can be obtained at www.ICGtesting.com
Printed in the USA
LVOW040803071011

249410LV00001B/5/P